T0339846

THE GLASS PALACE

THE GLASS PALACE

ILLUSIONS OF FREEDOM AND DEMOCRACY IN QATAR

NASSER M. BEYDOUN

&

JENNIFER BAUM

Algora Publishing
New York

Library of Congress Cataloging-in-Publication Data —

Beydoun, Nasser M.
   The glass palace: illusions of freedom and democracy in Qatar / Nasser M. Beydoun
and Jennifer Baum.
      p. cm.
   Includes bibliographical references and index.
   ISBN 978-0-87586-955-1 (alk. paper) — ISBN 978-0-87586-954-4 (pbk.: alk. paper)
— ISBN 978-0-87586-956-8 (ebk.: alk. paper) 1. Qatar—Politics and government. 2.
Qatar—Social conditions. 3. Qatar—Economic policy. 4. Qatar—Foreign economic
relations. I. Baum, Jennifer. II. Title.
   J699.C2B49 2012
   330.95363—dc23
                          2012032095

Printed in the United States

I dedicate this book to my wonderful wife Maysa, to my three wonderful children Aya, Jana and Mohamad Jamal, and to those family members, friends and colleagues who stood by us.

— Nasser M. Beydoun

TABLE OF CONTENTS

INTRODUCTION

The small emirate of Qatar has been playing a role in international affairs far greater in the past few years than one would expect. Qatar is about the size of Connecticut, with a native population estimated at just 250,000. It projects an enlightened, Westernized image while it is, in fact, a totalitarian regime operating under the guise of democracy.

But since 2007, Qatar has tapped its enormous gas reserves (the third largest reserves in the world, behind Russia and Iran) to become the largest exporter of liquefied natural gas (LNG) in the world. Gas revenues have given Qatar the highest per capita income in the world.

Qatar's international image is bolstered in part by the Al Jazeera news network based in Doha, the capital, and its successful (if controversial) bid to host the 2022 FIFA World Cup, the largest sporting event in the world. The country has sought to reinforce this image by hosting numerous international conferences and events. The image Qatar tries to project, however, is different than the reality on the ground.

Additionally, Qatar, with its newfound financial muscle, has been playing a significant role in the region's diplomatic arena, overshadowing the regional powerhouses of Saudi Arabia and Egypt—the countries who have traditionally been the regional mediators. Qatar's initiatives range from Darfur peace talks to Palestinian and Lebanese reconciliation, to possibly hosting U.S.-Taliban peace talks. Qatar helped forment the "revolution" that tore up Libya, and early on in the Libyan crisis, took a proactive position to bring about the downfall of the Gaddafi regime. Qatar was instrumental in providing NATO forces with the Arab political cover necessary to facilitate NATO's military involvement. The country assisted the transitional government financially and took an active role in marketing Libyan crude oil. Qatar attempted to leverage its involvement in Libya to gain an advantage in the post revolution economy. It also tried to interfere with the outcome of the political situation by investing billions of dollars to support hardline Muslim factions within the Libyan Transitional authorities. Even though Qatar remains active in Libya today, its influence has been greatly dimensioned. In the Syrian crisis, Qatar has played an even more brazen and destabilizing role. The Emir was among the first to call for the overthrow of the government in Syria, even though he enjoyed a close and deep friendship with Bashar Al Assad. Along with Saudi Arabia and with the blessing of the United States, Qatar has invested billions of dollars and provided military assistance to Free Syrian forces, with much of the funding going to hardline Islamic and Al Qaida affiliated factions. To this day, Qatar continues to play an oversized and aggressive role in the removal of the Assad regime.

This book aims to shed light on the grim reality that is Qatar today. It is written for everyone interested in knowing who America's allies are. Further, this book is for those who are considering working in Qatar, the Arab Gulf or another foreign country, especially one that uses an outdated work sponsorship system. We are often tempted by the financial rewards and excitement and adventure associated with moving to a foreign country, but we need to recognize the perils that exist and understand what consequences follow when things go wrong.

No one ever thinks anything bad will happen to him or herself, and I was no different. I never thought my experience in Qatar would end up the way it did, or that there were people as ruthless as those I dealt with while I was trapped. But there are, and this story shows them in action.

The title of this book, "The Glass Palace," comes from the old adage, "Those who live in glass houses shouldn't throw stones." Qatar portrays itself as a modern, tolerant society; it goes to great lengths and spends a lot of money to "promote democracy" throughout the Middle East. Yet it is a country that has no democracy at home, as it is ruled by an absolute monarch who overthrew his father to seize the throne.

To make things even worse, Qatar's labor laws make foreign workers virtual slaves to their Qatari masters. "Slave" is harsh terminology, but it is true, and you will hear the term used often among the many other workers trapped in Qatar against their will. It is not uncommon for Westerners holding white-collar jobs to be held hostage in Qatar after a work agreement has turned sour (my story as well as a few others will be detailed in this book), but unfortunately it is much more common for domestic or construction workers, most of whom come from Asia or the Indian subcontinent, to face this plight. With tight restrictions, no pay and no means to leave, it would be hard to say how they differ from slaves.

In the movie "Body of Lies," Hoffman, the CIA handler (played by Russell Crowe), says to Farris, the CIA Station Chief in Jordan (played by Leonardo DiCaprio), "No one likes the Middle East, because there is nothing to like." I make this statement with a heavy heart and deep remorse, for I spent most of my adult life working to change the image of the Arab world and Muslims in the United States. But unfortunately, this is the reality of the Arab world today. There truly is nothing to like. This is a region that is embroiled in war and ruled by totalitarian or sectarian regimes that for the most part put their own interests before those of their people. When democracy is introduced, it is always suffocated by confessional or tribal loyalties, which in turn creates new dictators and despots.

Despite its enormous achievements and contributions to civilization in past centuries, the Arab world has generally failed, over the last century and in recent history, to contribute anything to advance humanity. As a people, our main contribution in the last hundred years has been the flocks of emigrants who went to America and, to a lesser extent, Europe, fleeing famine, persecution and war. These people were able to achieve and contribute in their new societies. But it is not enough for the Arab world to remain stagnant while the population only takes comfort in the contributions Arabs made to civilization in the eighth and ninth centuries: in math, astronomy, architecture, medicine and more. They blame others for their problems, everyone from the Crusaders, to the Turks, to the Israelis, to the Americans. It is true that their natural resources have been exploited by European and American corporate interests, but their governments have been installed, often with outside interference, not for the benefit of their people but to subjugate those people for the sake of stability and to ensure uninterrupted access to oil.

This sad reality applies to the Middle East in general and the Arab world in particular. My experience was a tragedy to me and my family, yet I hope that by speaking out about it, I can effect change. We can effect change.

Chapter 1: An Economic Hostage in Qatar

On October 9, 2010, I drove my family to the airport to get them out of Doha and back to safety and a normal life in the United States. At that point, I had been held as a hostage in Qatar for a year, and there was no end in sight. I was uncertain when I would see my wife and kids again and had no idea how I, alone in Qatar, would be able to take on the Minister and his powerful family. But that day, all those apprehensions had to take the backseat to the task at hand: bidding my family goodbye.

I kissed Maysa, my wife, wiping the tears off her face. I tried to put on a brave front but I saw the uncertainty and fear in her eyes. She had been adamant that she did not want to leave me alone and split up the family, but I insisted. It is a father's instinct to get his family out of danger. Qatar was no longer safe for them or me. I did not want Maysa or the children to have to deal with any of the issues, stress or pressure I would be subjected to or when a knock would come to the door and I would be arrested. There was too much unknown for them to stay in Doha.

I kissed my oldest daughter, Aya, who would turn ten later that month. I admonished her to behave and listen to what her mother told her. Aya has a tendency to be mischievous, and she is smart beyond her years.

Then I kissed my daughter Jana. Aya was always my big girl, but Jana was my baby. She was small and looked frail, yet looks can be deceiving. Jana learned quickly that she could get me to do whatever she wanted by batting the lashes around her puppy dog hazel eyes. That day, she made me promise, a pinky promise, that I would be home in time for her eighth birthday on December 29, a promise I would be forced to break. She also made me promise I would let her have a dog, which she knew would never happen if it was up to her mother. I promised her a dog when I got back home.

I then picked up my son Jamal, and squeezed him as hard as possible without hurting him. I kissed him goodbye. The kisses seemed to have lasted an eternity. At three years old, Jamal had no idea what was happening around him. I knew that every day I was away from him, I was missing watching him grow and develop. He might be about to spend a majority of his young life without his father, but at the moment, he had no idea. He was happy to be going on a plane.

He hugged and kissed me and told me he loved me then jumped to his mother, eager to board the plane.

I watched as they passed airport immigration. I was waving at them and they were blowing kisses at me. The smile didn't leave my face until they disappeared into the crowds and I lost sight of them.

I can't describe the pain of seeing your family off and not knowing when you will be reunited with them. My heart felt like an anchor and my stomach was in knots. Tears began to cascade down my cheeks. I don't remember walking back to the car, but I know I sat in the airport parking lot for over an hour in despair and outrage.

I had never been so alone or felt so helpless; my future was no longer in my hands. My fate was to be determined by a system I didn't understand, in a country that just ten years earlier was a backwoods desert, a Third World country whose people were basically a composite of Wahhabis, unsophisticated Arab Bedouin tribes, Iranian traders, Palestinians, Egyptians and Sudanese, with a multitude of Indian and Pakistani clerks and shopkeepers and South Asian servants and labors.

This is not where I thought I would be when I moved to Qatar in April of 2007. I left Michigan a respected community leader, and just three and half years later, I was sitting in my car, having just bid my family goodbye—an economic hostage in Qatar.

There is a reason Qatar is particularly tempting to foreign workers, including me. In just over ten years, the country has seen dramatic and practically unheard of increases in population growth and per capita GDP. It has also been proactive in foreign policy and is driving expansion, a massive infrastructure upgrade and a shift in major industry through a "2030 National Vision Plan."

The rapid GDP growth alone is enough to put Qatar in the news and on the radar of any globally expanding business, but in order to understand Qatar today and how I got myself into this mess, some general context must be put into place.

1995: A New Qatar Begins to Take Shape

Perhaps the official start of today's Qatar came in 1995, when the current emir, Sheikh Hamad bin Khalifa al-Thani, unexpectedly overtook his father, Sheikh Khalifa Bin Hamad Bin Abdullah al-Thani, in a bloodless coup d'état. Sheikh Khalifa, who himself had seized power from an uncle in 1972, a year after Qatar gained independence from Great Britain, had been visiting Geneva, Switzerland at the time and vowed to return whatever the cost, calling the coup the "abnormal behavior of an ignorant man."[1]

However, soon afterward, senior members of the al Thani family gathered in Doha to pledge allegiance to Sheikh Hamad, and the United States recognized the new emir within days, after receiving assurances over its relations with Iran and Iraq.

The crown prince had, in effect, already been running the country for years, and to some degree the coup was a formality. Despite that, the following year Sheikh Khalifa, who was living in exile in France, staged an unsuccessful counter-coup. He remained exiled in France until he finally returned to Qatar in 2004. Today, the emir and his father are reconciled, though some supporters of the counter-coup staged against Sheikh Hamad in 1996 remain in prison.

After assuming power, Sheikh Hamad announced his intention for Qatar to move toward democracy and held municipal elections as a precursor to expected parliamentary elections, which are now planned for 2013. However, the elections have been postponed three times; most recently in June 2010, when the Emir extended the current unelected Consultative Assembly until 2013.

Qatari citizens approved a new constitution via public referendum in April 2003, and it came into force in June 2005. The country's constitution formalizes the hereditary rule of the al-Thani family, but it also establishes an elected legislative body and makes government ministers accountable to the legislature. In current practice, the emir's role is subject to influence by continuing traditions of consultation, rule by consensus,

---

1 Cockburn, Patrick. "Emir of Qatar deposed by his son." *The Independent* 28 Jun. 1995

and the citizen's right to appeal personally to the emir. The emir, while directly accountable to no one, cannot violate the Shari'a (Islamic law) and, in practice, must consider the opinions of leading families and the religious establishment.

STUNNING ECONOMIC AND POPULATION GROWTH

Who's Who in Qatar

Qatar is currently rated by the CIA as the fastest growing country in the world. The country's population has risen sharply over the past decade, from just under 600,000 in 2000 to an estimated 1.9 million in 2012. However, these population figures include the exorbitant numbers of foreign temporary workers; only about 15% hold Qatari citizenship. In other words, only about one in six people living in Qatar are actually Qatari citizens.

Thus the demographics do not spread out equally. Roughly 71% of the people in Qatar are male. *Gulf News* reported that in 2010, foreign workers represented 94.2% of the total economically active population in Qatar.[2]

Unsurprisingly, Qatar also claims the titles of highest population growth rate and highest net migration rate (the contribution of migration to the overall population change) in the world, by a large margin. According to CIA statistics, the net migration rate is nearly double that of Zimbabwe, which is second.

Alongside the population boom came staggering economic growth. Thanks to robust oil and natural gas reserves, Qatar has the highest per-capita income in the world. The country's GDP in 2011 was estimated to be $181.7 billion, but it is rated as having the fastest growing GDP in the world. Couple that with the fact that the country has the second lowest unemployment rate in the world (second only to Monaco) and it becomes a pretty appealing place to do business.

Prior to the boom and the bloodless coup, the oil revenue was the sole domain of the emir and the primary source of income of the government. The al-Thanis controlled most of the government ministries, while the Army was the bastion of the al-Attiyah family. Several local families dominated business in Qatar. These families were descendants of migrants from Iran, Bahrain and the Eastern Province of Saudi Arabia.

---

2   Toumi, Habib. "Qatar's Foreign Workers Overwhelm Labour Market." *The Gulf News* 24 Oct. 2011

In fact, before the bloodless coup, during the reign of Sheikh Khalifa, Qatar was a sleepy country and Doha, the capital, didn't see much growth from the 1960s until the after the mid-nineties. Prior to the discovery of oil, the country had few resources and the local population endured austere living conditions and a harsh climate. Famine commonly decimated the local population and forced others to migrate to neighboring areas.

Striking Oil

Early exploration for oil took place in 1935. The exploration, however, was adjourned due to border problems with the Kingdom of Saudi Arabia and Bahrain, but eventually started again, even more extensively, in 1938.

Oil was first discovered in Qatar in 1940 in Dukhan Field on the west coast. Early production averaged 5,000 barrels a day. Qatar was the fourth Gulf country, after Bahrain, Saudi Arabia and Kuwait, to begin production. Exploration was suspended during World War II, but resumed again in 1946.

In 1949, Qatar started to export oil through its Mesaieed port on the East Coast. In 1951, it reached 46,500 barrels a day—compared to only 34,000 a day before that time. The State of Qatar became number 11 among oil exporting countries in 1952, with a production of 67,700 barrels a day, i.e., 0.5% of world production.

A subsequent stage of oil investment in Qatar started in 1952 after an agreement with the Dutch Corporation Shell for the exploration of oil in Qatar's regional waters. Offshore production started in 1966 in the first discovered field al-Idd al-Sharqi, which was discovered in 1960, followed by Maydan Mahzam in 1963, and then the Abu al-Hanine field, which is the largest in production and in terms of the size of the reservoir. This led to the increase of Qatar's production to 233,000 barrels a day in 1965.

Independence

In 1971, Qatar won its independence from Britain and consequently assumed full control of the country's oil. In 1977, it nationalized all oil companies and handed over petrol investment to two main companies, Qatar Shell Limited and Qatar Oil Limited. In 1974, Qatar established the General Petroleum Corporation, known today as Qatar Petroleum, and gave it the responsibility of oil investment under the authority of Finance and Petrol Ministry at that time. In 1971, the discovery of North Gas Field, the largest single field in the world for natural non-associated gas, pushed Qatar's economy forward even further.

Understanding the Qatari Population

Qatari citizens can be divided into three groups: the Bedouin, Hadar, and Abd. The Bedouin descend from the nomads of the Arabian Peninsula, and the Hadar descend from settled town dwellers. While some Hadar are descendants of Bedouin, most descend from migrants from present-day Iran, Pakistan, and Afghanistan. The word "Alabd" translates to "slaves," and accordingly, this faction of the population are the descendants of slaves brought from east Africa. All three groups identify themselves as Qatari and their right to citizenship is not challenged.

Islam is the official religion in Qatar, and Islamic jurisprudence is the official basis of Qatar's legal system, although civil courts have jurisdiction over commercial law. Qatar is the only country other than Saudi Arabia to be dominated by the conservative Wahabi branch of Sunni Islam, and that includes the royal family of Qatar. While the majority of Qatari citizens are Sunni, 20% of the population identify with the Shi'a sect. This stems from the ancestral differences between the Bedouin and the Hadar; Qataris with ancestral links to Arabia are likely to identify with Bedouin cultural values and be adherents of Sunni Islam, whereas Qataris with ancestral links to regions along the northeastern side of the Gulf are likely to be adherents of Shi'a Islam.

After gaining independence from Great Britain in 1971, Qatar developed extensive social welfare programs for its citizens, including free health care, housing grants, and subsidized utilities. Education is compulsory from ages six to sixteen and free for all citizens through college. Because of this, Qatar has a high literacy rate. Institutions have also been established to support low-income families and disabled individuals through educational and job training programs.

Arabic is the official language, but English is more widely spoken, especially among foreign workers. Of the 85% non-Qatari population, about 25% are of other Arab nationality, 18% are Indian, 18% are Pakistani, 10% are Iranian, and 14% other. Foreign workers have no political rights. See chapter six for more information on foreign workers' rights and Qatar's work sponsorship system.

A Plan to Move Away from a Carbon-based Economy

Announced in 2008, Qatar's 2030 National Vision plan provides a broad social blueprint that aims to sow the seeds of a knowledge-based economy. The aim is for sustainable growth that does not rely on oil or liquefied natural gas. While the plan is no doubt admirable, one gets the sense that Qatar's PR machine is hard at work promoting a flashy concept with a deadline distant enough that no one really cares.

According to their plan, by 2030 Qatar aims to be an advanced society capable of sustaining its development and providing a high standard of living for its people. Qatar's National Vision defines the long-term outcomes for the country and provides a framework within which national strategies and implementation plans can be developed.

The National Vision addresses five major challenges facing Qatar: Modernization and preservation of traditions; Needs of this generation and the needs of future generations; Managed growth and uncontrolled expansion; Size and the quality of the expatriate labor force and the selected path of development; and Economic growth, social development and environmental management. And perhaps it is the section on environmental management that's most sorely needed; research released in 2011 by British risk analysis firm Maplecroft indicates that, based on the ratio of domestic, industrial and agricultural water consumption against renewable supplies of water from precipitation, rivers and groundwater, of the 17 countries designated as being "extreme risk" of experiencing an interruption to its water supply, Qatar was ranked second.[3] Yet, despite this grim news, per capita household water use in Qatar is one of the highest in the world.[4]

The plan foresees development through four interconnected pillars:

1. Human Development: development of all its people to enable them to sustain a prosperous society;

2. Social Development: development of a just and caring society based on high moral standards, and capable of playing a significant role in global partnerships for development;

3. Economic Development: development of a competitive and diversified economy capable of meeting the needs of, and securing a high standard of living for, all its people both for the present and for the future;

4. Environmental Development: management of the environment such that there is harmony between economic growth, social development and environmental protection.

3 "World's Most Water Stressed Countries: Bahrain, Qatar, Yemen Facing Extreme Shortages." *Huffington Post.* 19 May 2011.
4 "Qatar tops per capita water use in world." *The Peninsula.* 30 Mar. 2011.

In a report on the Qatar National Vision 2030, Sheikha Mozah Bint Nasser al-Missned, the second of the three wives of Sheikh Hamad, stressed the importance of education as of one of the key components that enables Qatar's people and institutions, including the Qatar Foundation, to bring development and happiness. The Qatar Foundation was established in 1995 by Sheikh Hamad. Today it is Qatar's driving force in its journey from a carbon economy to a knowledge-based economy. Sheikha Mozah is the organization's chairperson. See chapter three for more information on education in Qatar or the appendix for a deeper look at the Western universities opening campuses in Qatar.

Setting the Stage for 2022's World Cup

A surprise choice for the 2022 World Cup, today the once obscure oil- and natural gas-rich Gulf nation is a household name to soccer fans around the world. Qatar lacks the stadiums, infrastructure and optimal weather conditions that would normally be required of the host country by the FIFA Executive Committee. Despite that, Qatar is to become the first Arab country to host what is the largest single sport event in the world.

In its bid for the event (expected to draw around half a million visitors), Qatar promised FIFA officials it would spend whatever necessary to make the World Cup a success, and in doing so it beat out four other bidders: Australia, Japan, South Korea and the United States.

Qatar is already fully entrenched in an ambitious "National Vision" plan, as noted. Included in this plan are significant projects for expanding and updating infrastructure, the timing of which has been sped up to accommodate hosting the World Cup. Qatar will enjoy the added benefit of upgraded sports facilities and the addition of more luxury hotel rooms, which were not included in the vision plan before.

The bestowment of the hosting privilege was a shock to many people worldwide; most news analysts thought the country didn't stand a chance.

The World Cup is awarded based on a voting system by the twenty-four member FIFA executive committee. Shortly after Qatar was awarded the tournament, allegations were made that the country had entered into a vote-sharing agreement with Spain, which is not allowed under FIFA rules. This was followed by claims in the *Sunday Times* newspaper by a supposed whistleblower that two African FIFA executive committee members, Issa Hayatou and Jacques Anouma, had been paid bribes to vote for Qatar. Hayatou, Anouma, and Qatar all denied the claims, and the whistleblower has since come forward and stated that his claims were false.

The scandal coincided with the election of the FIFA president. Current President Sepp Blatter won reelection after his only rival, Qatar's Mohamed bin Hammam, was suspended, then expelled, in an investigation into allegations of bribery.

FIFA vice president Jack Warner was suspended at the same time, pending the outcome of the investigation of corruption allegations. He ultimately resigned, but he responded to the suspension by leaking an email from FIFA secretary general Jerome Valcke, in which he wrote of Bin Hammam: "I never understood why he was running [for president]. If really he thought he had a chance, or ... he thought you can buy FIFA as they bought the World Cup."

Valcke has since denied he was referring to any unethical behavior, and FIFA has repeatedly denied there is any need for an investigation into the awarding of the World Cup to Qatar.

Qatar had in fact submitted the lowest-ranked technical bid; FIFA's technical inspectors rated the offer as a "high overall operational risk," making it the only one of the nine bids for the 2018 and 2022 tournaments to be judged anything other than a low or medium risk. This reflected concerns about hosting the tournament in a country with temperatures that can reach 122 degrees Fahrenheit in the summer, when the games are scheduled to be held.

But what Qatar couldn't offer in practicality, it made up for in panache.

Their bid included 12 state-of-the-art carbon-neutral stadiums. Nine are to be built from scratch, and three others are already-existing stadiums that are to be renovated. In a move that resolves the logistical problem of maintaining stadiums that would sit empty post event while at the same time displaying neighborly brotherhood, after the World Cup the stadiums are to be disassembled and the parts used for twenty-two new stadiums in developing countries (a significantly less carbon-neutral endeavor that the developing countries may or may not be able to afford and maintain).

Qatar's win was partly based on the guarantee of air-conditioning within the stadiums to keep temperatures at comfortable levels—quite a feat for venues seating upwards of 50,000 people in the scorching desert sun. And they said they'd do it in a carbon-neutral way.

The proposed designs included in the bid are too fantastical not to mention.

First, the Doha Port Stadium would be situated on an artificial peninsula built in the Persian Gulf. Water from the Gulf would also run around the outer part of the building and double as a natural cooling system, a.k.a a 21st-century moat that provides air conditioning as it evaporates. Water would be the building's primary energy source, and visitors could be taken to the stadium by water taxis.

While the Port Stadium may arguably be the most impressive, the others certainly have noteworthy features. The al-Gharrafa Stadium, which was initially built in 2003, will undergo a major renovation. The outer part of the stadium will be covered in ribbons representing the nations who qualify for the 2022 World Cup—to promote unity.

The al-Rayyan stadium features an outer wrap-around membrane that will be used as a screen to display advertisements, live scores, match updates and replays, allowing people to watch games from outside the stadium—if they can stand the heat.

The architects incorporated many cultural aspects into the state-of-the-art designs of the other stadiums, including seashells, traditional-style Arabian forts, pearl diving, Arab tents, and fishing. The concepts must be seen to be appreciated.

The advanced air conditioning system would work like this: Solar thermal collectors and photovoltaic panels on the outside and the roofs of the stadiums will harness energy from the unforgiving Qatari sun. The energy will be used to chill water (the Gulf can reach 100°F in summer), which in turn will cool air before it is blown through the stadium, keeping temperatures below 80°F. The photovoltaic panels would also export electricity to Qatar's national grid, which would make the cooling system carbon neutral.

Not long after the bid was awarded, this elaborate air conditioning plan was dismissed by one of the architects, John Barrow of the firm Populous, who said that air conditioning on such a scale is 'notoriously unsustainable.' "We are doing away with all the air conditioning kit that is going to cost a fortune to run," Barrow told delegates at the International Football Arena conference in Zurich.[5]

Barrow noted the plan may now rely on more traditional Arab methods, including wind towers that assist ventilation by sucking up hot air and improving circulation.

---

5   "Qatar World Cup stadium designer tells 2022 hosts air conditioned stadiums must be scrapped." *Daily Mail Online.* 8 Nov. 2011

However, after Barrow's comments, organizers in Qatar said there is no intention to scrap the original plans.

In any case, it's going to be an expensive endeavor. Qatar plans to spend $4 billion on stadium infrastructure alone, and the country is pouring tens of billions of dollars into transportation infrastructure as part of a broader overhaul. Overall, it has been estimated they will spend a total of $220 billion. In comparison, South Africa spent $5 billion in total on hosting the 2010 World Cup, which generated $4 billion in revenue.

Although all elements of the futuristic stadiums may or may not come to fruition, other sci-fi-like ideas are being considered, such as large, robotic cloud-like structures to cool the stadiums. The "clouds" would be made from a lightweight carbon structure and kept aloft by four solar-powered engines to be controlled remotely. The space-age awnings can be produced for a mere $500,000 each.

All jokes aside, this level of innovation and economic commitment means plenty of business and job opportunities.

George Nasra, the managing director of International Bank of Qatar, has said Qatar anticipates significant opportunity for a range of industries during the preparations leading up to the World Cup, including contracting companies, design firms, real estate companies and financing companies, among others. Locally, the World Cup will primarily create jobs for transient foreign workers, rather than Qataris, and produce contracts for foreign contractors who will be importing building materials.

Qatar is on a roll and does not plan to stop with the 2022 World Cup; Doha is also currently an applicant for the 2020 Summer Olympics. Whether it becomes a candidate had not been decided at press time.

Qatar is growing fast and will likely continue to do so, as it vies for international prestige and recognition. Short-run employment usually increases by 15 to 25 percent as a result of major international sporting events, according to the Brookings Institution. The race to complete the stadiums and their accompanying gadgets and infrastructure will no doubt mean even more foreign workers will flood Qatar in the next ten years. It is crucial for any non-Qatari business or worker to understand the full implications of doing business in Qatar. The time is now to bring Qatar's outdated work sponsorship system into the light.

Chapter 2: A Wannabe Superpower: Qatar's Political and Military Involvement throughout the Middle East

The tiny nation of Qatar is turning into a major international player at an astonishing rate. Historically, Egypt and Saudi Arabia have been the regional powerhouses; they stepped in as mediators during times of conflict throughout the Middle East. Both support the Middle East peace process and have been key partners in the resolution of the Israeli–Palestinian conflict.

But while Egypt's government is in transition and Saudi Arabia is dealing with its own civil unrest (mostly coming from the Eastern Province, which has a border with Qatar), Qatar's prominence and economy continue to grow. Without any threats or disturbances facing Qatar today, Sheikh Hamad has been free to get involved in political affairs throughout the Middle East, and indeed, especially in the past decade, Qatar's foreign policy has shifted. Qatar has become a proactive mediator throughout the region.

Compared to other countries in the region, Qatar has another specific advantage that has allowed it to take on a more proactive role in the region: mainly, the fact that Qatar's security is guaranteed by the United States via the huge al-Udeid U.S. Air Force base, which has the longest runway in the Middle East, and Camp As Sayliyah, which is the U.S. military's largest pre-positioning base outside of the continental United States.[6]

---

6   Roberts, David. "Behind Qatar's Intervention in Libya." *Foreign Affairs* 28 Sept. 2011

According to a March 2012 article in *Der Spiegel*, "Doha's diplomatic district is in the process of turning into a kind of miniature international organization, where the forces of good and evil alike are permitted to hoist their flags. Secular opponents of the Somali al-Shabab militants, deposed Iraqi generals and members of the Egyptian Muslim Brotherhood have found refuge there. The emir urged the Palestinian organization Hamas to move its headquarters from the Syrian capital Damascus to Doha. Hamas leader Khaled Mashaal already maintains a residence in Qatar, and the Taliban will soon open an office in Doha—its first representation in a foreign country."[7]

The Arab Spring that swept the region in 2011 provided further opportunity for Qatar to use its time and money to shape the region, and in fact, the emir's role changed with the Arab Spring: he has gone from being a mediator to a political player.[8] In May, the Qatari government hosted its 11th annual Doha Forum, a conference about democracy and free trade, with the theme of 'Enriching the Middle East's Economic Future.' The conference featured an opening session about the revolutions that have rocked the Arab world.

Qatar's Crown Prince Sheikh Tamim bin Hamad al-Thani opened the Doha Forum and said that the yearning for freedom neither contradicts the Arab culture and identity nor opposes the tenets of Islam as a religion and civilization. He also noted that the Arab revolutions have proved that Arab youth are not "spoiling themselves in the evils of consumer life."[9]

Since the mid-1990s, Qatar has pursued an activist foreign policy, using its affluence, unthreatening military position and skills as a mediator to interject itself in conflicts around the Middle East and beyond.[10] Since the Arab spring, however, the country has taken a more aggressive regional role, most notably over Libya.[11]

Indeed, Qatar has played a large role in all of the Arab uprisings we witnessed in 2011; and even before then, the country involved itself in other conflicts throughout the Middle East region. Below is a summary

7   Smoltczyk, Alexander and Zand, Bernhard. "Tiny Qatar has Big Diplomatic Ambitions." *Der Spiegel* 14 Mar. 2012

8   Smoltczyk, Alexander and Zand, Bernhard. "Tiny Qatar has Big Diplomatic Ambitions." *Der Spiegel* 14 Mar. 2012

9   "Doha Forum Highlights Reforms in the Arab World." *Khaleej Times* 9 May 2011

10   Roberts, David. "Behind Qatar's Intervention in Libya." *Foreign Affairs* 28 Sept. 2011

11   Beaumont, Peter. "Qatar Accused of Interfering in Libyan Affairs." *The Guardian* 4 Oct. 2011

of Qatar's involvement in a few countries throughout the region over the past decade or so.

LEBANON

Well before the Arab Spring, Qatar played a prominent role during the 2006 conflict between Hezbollah, a Shi'a Muslim militant group and political party based in Lebanon, and Israel. In short, the conflict began when Hezbollah militants killed three Israeli soldiers and kidnapped two others in a bid to negotiate a prisoner exchange, which was rebuffed by Israel. Another five Israeli soldiers were killed after the ambush, and Israel responded by bombing hundreds of targets in Lebanon, including Beirut's airport and Hezbollah's headquarters in southern Beirut, and setting up a naval blockade. Hezbollah responded with rocket attacks targeting northern Israeli cities.[12]

Thirty-four days later, in August, a cease-fire brokered by the United Nations ended hostilities. About 1,000 people, mostly Lebanese civilians, were killed, and 1 million Lebanese civilians and some 300,000 to 400,000 Israelis were temporarily displaced. Both countries' economies suffered, although Lebanon's suffered far more as much of its infrastructure—roads, bridges, electricity and water plants—was damaged by Israel's bombing campaign.

Qatar provided a small number of troops to the UN's peacekeeping mission in Lebanon after the Israeli bombing. Qatar also quickly sent relief supplies and financial aid to Lebanon. This financial investment in Lebanon helped Qatar in gaining Hezbollah support for Qatari involvement in the country. It allowed Lebanese to come to Qatar and seek employment, swelling their numbers in Qatar to over sixty thousand. And the Emir was the first Arab head of state to visit Beirut, immediately after the cessation of hostilities.

After the war, Sheikh Hamad spoke of Hezbollah's "victory" over the Israelis and provided millions of dollars to help rebuild four heavily bombed Hezbollah villages. The move went a long way in furthering Lebanese support for Qatari intervention.

The claim of resistance and victory against Israel went against what other powers in the region were saying—their implications were that Hezbollah had triggered the war.

Soon after the conflict, Lebanon fell into a long political stalemate, as the country was without a head of state after November of 2007, when

---

12 "Timeline: Decades of Conflict in Lebanon, Israel." *CNN* 14 Jul. 2006

Syrian-backed incumbent Emile Lahoud left office at the end of his term. In Lebanon, the president is required to be a Maronite Christian, the prime minister a Sunni, and the Speaker of the parliament a Shi'a.

In 2008, Qatar mediated a successful power-sharing deal to break the 18-month-long political stalemate in Lebanon.[13] Sheikh Hamad chaired six days of Arab League talks in Doha that ended with a deal between the United States-backed ruling coalition and the Hezbollah-led opposition.

Sheikh Hamad was lauded internationally for his success after leaders from other countries had tried and failed. The *L.A. Times* went as far as to say Sheikh Hamad "emerged as a diplomatic rock star."[14]

At the time, Qatar had close ties to and credibility with Iran, Syria and Saudi Arabia[15] (which not many other countries were able to boast), and this made the breakthrough a "victory" for Arab diplomacy.

In 2010, Sheikh Hamad became the first Arab leader to tour South Lebanon and view the various projects Qatar had funded following the 2006 war. He also inaugurated a hospital in Bint Jbeil (my ancestral village), Lebanon, and a nearby mosque and church, while accompanied by Lebanon's President Michel Sleiman and Prime Minister Saad al-Hariri.

As recently as March of 2012, Qatar was still actively working to form strong diplomatic ties with Lebanon. Lebanese President Michel Sleiman visited Doha for a conference on poverty that month, and he and Sheikh Hamad discussed boosting bilateral cooperation in various fields.[16]

ISRAEL

In 2007, Sheikh Hamad took a bold step in becoming the first Persian Gulf ruler to meet with a high-ranking Israeli official to pursue peace negations in an attempt to further Qatar's image as a neutral and peaceful regional power. However, in January of 2009, Qatar, the sole Gulf state to have trade ties with Israel, finally cut ties after Palestinians had endured months of blockades in Gaza. Interestingly, although the head of the Israeli delegation in Doha had been ordered to leave, the Qatari authorities allowed the delegation's offices to remain open in order not to

13 Roberts, David. "Behind Qatar's Intervention in Libya." *Foreign Affairs* 28 Sept. 2011

14 "Lebanon: Qatar Emerges as Diplomatic Powerhouse." *Los Angeles Times* 15 May 2008

15 "Lebanon: Qatar Emerges as Diplomatic Powerhouse." *Los Angeles Times* 15 May 2008

16 "Lebanon, Qatar Discuss Boosting Bilateral Cooperation." *The Daily Star* 6 Mar. 2012

totally end the relationship. In March of the same year, however, Israel took the initiative to sever ties and closed the office.

Before that move, despite Qatar's clear support of Hezbollah and influx of cash into Lebanon after the 2006 conflict between Israel and Hezbollah, Qatar had maintained an active relationship with Israel, albeit one that was sometimes difficult to understand.

Assistant Professor of History and author of *Qatar: A Modern History*, Allen J. Fromherz, asserts the importance of the relationship between Qatar and its U.S. military protector cannot be underestimated, and it may be that relationship that is ultimately influencing Qatar's relations with Israel. "Qatar's abrupt repudiation of its relations with Israel in January 2009 may have had more to do with the changing political landscape in the USA—the inauguration of a U.S. President less reflexively supportive of Israel (Barack Obama)—than the humanitarian crisis in Gaza. After all, Qatar had maintained its relationship with Israel throughout the humanitarian crisis of the Second Intifada but a very different U.S. administration was then in power," Fromherz writes.

However, once the international and regional condemnation of Israeli actions in Gaza lessened, Qatar attempted to reestablish its ties with Israel in 2009 and 2010. This time, however, the Qatari initiative was met with a clear rebuttal from the Prime Minister Benyamin Netanyahu and the Foreign Minister Avigdor Lieberman.

Israel's citizens are banned from Qatar, as they are from most Gulf States, so what does that mean for the 2022 World Cup? Chief Executive of the Qatar 2022 World Cup bid, Hassan Abdulla al Thawadi, said Qatar would let Israel take part in the World Cup, despite not recognizing the Jewish state. Such an invitation would be unprecedented in the Arab world.

SUDAN

Prior to the Arab Spring, Qatar was already beginning to flex its diplomatic muscles in Sudan. The largest and one of the most geographically diverse states in Africa, Sudan split into two countries in July of 2011 after the people of the south voted for independence. This followed two rounds of north–south civil war that cost the lives of 1.5 million people.[17] The continuing conflict in the western region of Darfur has driven two million people from their homes and killed more than 200,000.[18]

---

17 "Sudan Profile." *BBC News* 1 May 2012
18 "Sudan Profile." *BBC News* 1 May 2012

The Darfur Conflict began in February 2003 when the Sudan Liberation Movement/Army and Justice and Equality Movement groups in Darfur took up arms, accusing the Sudanese government of oppressing non-Arab Sudanese in favor of Sudanese Arabs.

Qatar has sought to serve as a mediator between the Sudanese government and various rebels groups in the Darfur peace process, and several peace negotiations took place in Doha, Qatar, nearly 2,000 miles away from the conflict, beginning in 2009. In July of 2011, a peace agreement was signed by the Government of Sudan and the Liberation and Justice Movement.

Qatar's involvement in the Darfur crisis is an example of the country stepping into what would have normally been mediated by Egypt, which borders Sudan to the north and has long been involved in Sudanese affairs. In fact, prior to 2009, according to the Middle East Media Research Institute, "Egypt and Qatar were engaged in a power struggle over mediation of the Darfur crisis. In September 2008, at Syrian President Bashar al-Assad's suggestion, the Arab League and the African Union appointed Qatar to sponsor negotiations between the Darfur rebels and the Sudanese government. Qatar, however, was able to bring only one of the Sudanese rebel organizations to the negotiations table—the Justice and Equality Movement. Following the first round of negotiations, in Doha, the Sudanese government and the Justice and Equality Movement signed a goodwill agreement; the agreement, however, was never implemented."[19]

The article goes on to surmise that for Qatar, "the mediation of the Darfur conflict was a means of gaining prestige and recognition as a key player in Middle East and international diplomacy. Thus, the Qatari government daily *al-Raya* termed Qatar's mediation of the Darfur conflict a success, completely disregarding Egypt's initiatives: 'Qatar has achieved a significant breakthrough, since all sides in Sudan responded to its earnest efforts to organize the next round of peace negotiations aimed at resolving the Darfur crisis—something that can be accomplished only by [the Sudanese themselves]... Qatar's efforts will definitely continue; they will not cease until [all] the sides in Sudan reach a comprehensive resolution of the Darfur crisis...'"[20]

But in 2011, the Qatar News Agency reported that Egypt welcomed the signing of the Darfur peace agreement and expressed appreciation

---

19   Green, R. "Solving the Darfur Crisis: The U.S. Prefers Qatar to Egypt as Mediator." *The Middle East Media Research Institute* 19 Aug. 2009

20   Green, R. "Solving the Darfur Crisis: The U.S. Prefers Qatar to Egypt as Mediator." *The Middle East Media Research Institute* 19 Aug. 2009

for the efforts made by the State of Qatar over the years to achieve this important step.[21]

According to Qatar's news agency, in March of 2012 Qatar pledged to invest $2 billion in Sudan, following a visit from the Sudanese president Omar al-Bashir. The reports suggest that Qatar will buy Sudanese bonds and may also consider investing in the nation's mining, oil and agriculture industries.[22] Sudan's economy has been struggling since South Sudan gained independence and took with it most of the country's oil production.[23]

Bashir has traveled frequently to Qatar. It should be noted that Bashir has been indicted for war crimes, crimes against humanity, and genocide by the International Criminal Court[24], and in Darfur, the United Nations has accused pro-government Arab militias of a campaign of ethnic cleansing against non-Arab locals.[25]

YEMEN

Yemen is the poorest country in the Middle East, with a severe shortage of water and rising levels of malnutrition among its population of about 25 million.

In recent years, Qatar has facilitated temporary agreements between the Yemeni government and the Houthi rebels[26], a Zaidi Shi'a insurgent group operating in Yemen. The Zaydi Shi'a have a unique approach within Shi'a Islamic thought that results in similarities to orthodox Sunni Islam.

But Qatar and Yemen have long had a troubled relationship, and the unrest in Yemen that began in 2011 as the population got caught up in the Arab Spring and began calling for an end to then-President Ali Abdullah Saleh's 33-year rule began to change the narrative of Qatar's involvement.

A few months after the uprising began, Qatar pressed Saleh to sign a Gulf power transfer deal.[27]

21 "Egyptian FM Hails Qatar's Role in Darfur Peace Process." *The Consulate General of the State of Qatar, Houston* 14 July 2011

22 "Qatar Pledges to Invest $2 bn in Sudan." *AFP* 7 Mar. 2012

23 "Qatar Pledges to Invest $2 bn in Sudan." *AFP* 7 Mar. 2012

24 "Sudan's Defense Minister Wanted for War Crimes." *CNN* 2 Mar. 2012

25 "Sudan Profile." *BBC News* 1 May 2012

26 Roberts, David. "Behind Qatar's Intervention in Libya." *Foreign Affairs* 28 Sept. 2011

27 "Qatar Presses Yemen's Saleh on Power Transfer Deal." *Reuters Africa* 17 Nov. 2011

Yemen's transition to a new president was being brokered by the six-nation Gulf Cooperation Council, which is made up of Bahrain, Kuwait, Oman, Qatar, Saudi Arabia and the United Arab Emirates.

In early April, the Qatari prime minister publicly called for the resignation of Saleh—a statement that departed from the more conciliatory position of other Gulf nations and led Saleh to charge that Qatar "has conspired against Yemen."[28]

It should be noted that Qatar's alliances change from country to country and from crisis to crisis. On Libya, Qatar cooperated with Saudi Arabia to get rid of Gaddafi, their common enemy. When Sheikh Hamad noticed that the king of Saudi Arabia was not as determined as he was to convince then Yemeni President Ali Abdullah Saleh to step down, he quit the negotiations and left it up to Washington to apply pressure on the Saudis.[29]

In an announcement carried by the state news agency QNA, Qatar said the decision was made "because of procrastination and delay in signing the agreement proposed in the initiative" and "the continued escalation and confrontations and the loss of wisdom, which is incompatible with the spirit of the initiative."[30]

In response, Yemen recalled its ambassador from Qatar and the Yemeni government said it "warmly welcomed" Qatar's withdrawal from negotiations.[31] The Yemeni government also accused the Gulf state of "funding chaos" and the Qatar-based Al Jazeera television network of supporting protests against the president.[32]

The relationship between Qatar and Saleh's government was further deteriorated when Saleh told Russia Today television that "The state of Qatar is funding chaos in Yemen and in Egypt and Syria and throughout the Arab world." Saleh also accused Al Jazeera, which is funded by Qatar's government, of provoking the protests.[33]

But in November, Qatar was again pressuring Saleh to sign a power transfer deal "without delay" after prolonged protests against his rule.[34]

---

28 Eakin, Hugh. "The Strange Power of Qatar." *The New York Review of Books* 27 Oct. 2011

29 Smoltczyk, Alexander and Zand, Bernhard. "Tiny Qatar has Big Diplomatic Ambitions." *Der Spiegel* 14 Mar. 2012

30 "Qatar Bails out of Yemen Pact, Citing 'Procrastination'." *CNN* 12 May 2011

31 "Yemen: Qatar Withdraws Support for GCC Agreement; Expert Warns of Violence." *LA Times* 13 May 2011

32 "Qatar Pulls out of Yemen Crisis Mediation." *Financial Times* 13 May 2011

33 "Qatar Withdraws from Yemen Mediation Bid." *Aljazeera* 13 May 2011

34 "Qatar Presses Yemen's Saleh on Power Transfer Deal." *Reuters* 17 Nov. 2011

He finally did at the end of November, and a year after the revolution began, longtime vice president Abed Rabbo Mansour Hadi was elected president in a one-man race. He has promised to hold a referendum within 18 months on a new constitution.

TUNISIA

Demonstrations beginning in Tunisia in December of 2010 were precipitated by high unemployment, food inflation, corruption, a lack of freedom of speech and other political freedoms and poor living conditions. The protests were sparked by the self-immolation of Mohamed Bouazizi, whose act became a catalyst for the Tunisian Revolution and the wider Arab Spring. His drastic measure incited demonstrations and riots throughout Tunisia in protest of social and political issues in the country and eventually led to the ousting of President Zine El Abidine Ben Ali 28 days later on January 14, 2011, when he officially resigned after 23 years in power.

Compared to the bloodshed in Syria and Libya, the uprising to overthrow Ben Ali in January last year was largely peaceful.

Qatar supported the overthrow of Ben Ali, and in Tunisia, no other Internet or broadcast medium did more to spread the cause of popular protest than Al Jazeera, Qatar's government-backed satellite television news network.

Al Jazeera and its sister site Al Jazeera English were first on the scene with insightful and bold reports, the likes of which hadn't been seen before. Coverage was so good, first of the Tunisia uprising, and then the subsequent Egypt and Libya uprisings, that U.S. Secretary of State Hillary Clinton stood before a Senate Foreign Relations committee in May of 2011 and said the network was "changing peoples' minds and attitudes... like it or hate it, it is really effective."

Unlike Egypt, in the year following the uprising, Tunisia was able to move forward and hold elections of its own.

The Islamist political party, Ennahda, claimed victory in Tunisia's elections, which were the first elections to follow the popular uprisings of the Arab Spring. Originally inspired by the Muslim Brotherhood in Egypt, Ennahda advocates a more overtly Islamic identity and society for the country. Ennahda's growth has included new offices all over the country paid for by Qatar, according to rumors that have not been confirmed by officials in the party.[35] The rumors of outside support of the Islamist party have fueled anxiety among some largely urban, secularist Tunisians.

In January of 2012, one year after the start of the Arab Spring, Sheikh Hamad and Tunisian Interim Prime Minister Beji Caid Essebsi chaired a session of talks between Qatar and Tunisia aimed to strengthen "brotherly ties" between the two nations. *Gulf News* reports that "Talks dealt with ways to strengthen the 'relations between the two countries in various fields as well as a number of regional and international issues of common interest'."[36]

The news outlet went on to report that after the meeting, the emir and the Tunisian prime minister witnessed the signing of agreements and memorandums of understanding between the two countries. These included an agreement on investing in Tunisian Treasury bonds, a memorandum of understanding to explore investment prospects in environmental preservation and supporting the efforts to combat pollution and memos on vocational training as well for co-operation in oil refining and a natural gas network program for Tunisian cities between Qatar Petroleum International and the Tunisian government.

In addition, a draft memorandum of understanding on cooperation between Qatar Electricity and Water Company and the Tunisian Electricity and Gas Company and a memorandum between Qatar National Bank and the Tunisian finance ministry were also signed.

It doesn't stop there; *Gulf News* also reported that an investment agreement to develop a project for equipping the railway station in Soussa as well as the extension of a memorandum of understanding on the Mahdia Town Project were signed by Qatari Diar Real Estate Investment Company and the Tunisian government.

Following the talks, the Tunisian prime minister expressed the hope that the emir's visit would "support Tunisia's development plan and expand relations between the two countries' peoples."[37]

Also one year after the Arab Spring, Bloomberg reported that Tunisian Central Bank Governor Mustapha Kamel Nabli said his country

35 Eshelby, Kate. "Tunisia: A Year on from the Revolution." *The Metro* 6 Mar. 2012

36 "Qatar, Tunisia Sign Investment Accords." *Gulf Times* 14 Jan. 2012

37 "Qatar, Tunisia Sign Investment Accords." *Gulf Times* 14 Jan. 2012

may sell $500 million in dollar-denominated treasury bills to Qatar, as it seeks to secure about $5 billion in external financing this year.[38]

While not directly involved during the uprising itself, Qatar has played and continues to play a large role in reshaping Tunisia today as the country undergoes massive reform.

EGYPT

Inspired by the Tunisian uprising and mobilized on social media sites Facebook and Twitter, thousands of Egyptians converged on Cairo's central Tahrir Square on January 25, 2011 to call for President Hosni Mubarak's removal from office. The protest—dubbed a "day of revolution against torture, poverty, corruption and unemployment"[39]—began peacefully, but as the crowd grew, security forces changed tactics and police fired tear gas and rubber bullets, prompting clashes.

Within a week, the number of protesters on Tahrir Square increased to a quarter-million. Less than two weeks later, it was announced that Mubarak would resign and turn over power to the military, along with the promise that the army won't act as a substitute for a government based on the "legitimacy of the people."[40] Fireworks burst over Tahrir Square while the world watched.

Similar to what happened in Tunisia; Al Jazeera played a crucial role in promulgating the protest.

Under former president Hosni Mubarak, Qatar had strained relations with Egypt. However, since Mubarak's February 11, 2011 ousting, Qatar was one of the first countries to support Egypt's new government and has increasingly gotten more involved in Egyptian affairs. It is important to note that Egypt has the largest population in the Middle East, with over 81 million people.

Egypt's economy had been rapidly growing before the popular uprising, but it was hit hard by the protests, leading foreign investors to withdraw funds. Other major revenue sources, such as tourism, suffered.

In October of 2011 it was announced by Egypt's Finance Minister, Hazem el-Beblawi, that Qatar had given a grant of $500 million to Egypt to support its budget, which had ballooned as a result of political turmoil. El-Beblawi had been negotiating with other Gulf Arab states for financial

---

38   Shahine, Alaa. "Tunisia May Sell Debt to Qatar, Needs $5 Billion Financing." *Bloomberg* 27 Jan. 2012
39   "A Look at How Egypt's Uprising Unfolded." *Associated Press* 11 Feb. 2011
40   "A Look at How Egypt's Uprising Unfolded." *Associated Press* 11 Feb. 2011

assistance as well. According to Reuters, Hazem el-Beblawi said he was negotiating with Saudi Arabia and the United Arab Emirates for funds worth close to $7 billion. He also said he was considering International Monetary Fund financing that Egypt previously turned down.[41]

Khalid al-Attiyah, Qatar's minister of state for international cooperation, told Al Jazeera satellite channel that Qatar's aim was to offer direct support for the budget and loans at very low rates to deal with the immediate economic issues, as well as to offer investment.

The minister mentioned two projects in port cities, one in Port Saeed and the other in Alexandria. "These two projects will provide hundreds of thousands of job opportunities," al-Attiyah said.[42]

A few months before the announcement, Egypt's Minister of Planning and International Cooperation Fayza Abouelnaga said in a press statement, after meeting with the Qatari Minister of State for Foreign Affairs, Khalid al-Attiyah, that both ministers discussed the Qatari financial aid package.

"We discussed various areas of development and investment cooperation between Egypt and Qatar, and the mutual visits, especially the visit of his highness the Emir of the State of Qatar to Cairo, the visit of the Egyptian Prime Minister to Doha, as well as the multiple visits of the Qatari international cooperation minister to Egypt," said Abouelnaga.[43]

Abouelnaga said the investments were expected to be in sectors including tourism, housing, oil, transport, agriculture, education, health and justice.[44]

The Egypt Independent noted that, "Some activists fear that the monetary intervention of Gulf States in the state budget could have political implications in the country's current democratic transition."[45] The same article also referenced the Kuwaiti *al-Watan* newspaper, which, the month before, had quoted sources as saying that Gulf States are mulling potential membership of Egypt in the Gulf Cooperation Council. "Crit-

---

41 "Egypt says Qatar Gave $500 mln to Help with Budget." *Reuters Africa* 9 Oct. 2011

42 "Egypt says Qatar Gave $500 mln to Help with Budget." *Reuters Africa* 9 Oct. 2011

43 Azouz, Mohamed. "Qatar Supports Egypt's General Budget with US$500 Million, Increases Investments." *Egypt Independent* 6 Oct. 2011

44 "Qatar Pledges $10 bln Investment in Egpyt." *AFP* 28 May 2011

45 Azouz, Mohamed. "Qatar Supports Egypt's General Budget with US$500 Million, Increases Investments." *Egypt Independent* 6 Oct. 2011

ics view the move as an attempt by the Gulf to expand its power in the region," the article states.[46]

LIBYA

Following the protests, unrest and confrontations that began in Libya in February of 2011 and led to civil war and ultimately the capture and killing of Muammar Gaddafi in October of 2011, Qatar was instrumental in securing the support of the Arab League for the NATO intervention that began in March of 2011. Qatar contributed its own military aircraft to the mission and was the only Arab state to actively join in NATO operations. But Qatar also gave $400 million to the rebels, helped them market Libyan oil out of Benghazi, and set up a TV station for them in Doha.[47]

The state-of-the-art Libya TV studios were established in the early days of the conflict to counter the "propaganda" being broadcast on Libyan state TV by supporters of Muammar Gaddafi, in other words, the standing government. The rebels' network was launched in just five days, with no dry runs or practice. Dozens of Libyan journalists and non-journalists alike were recruited and trained at lightning speed to launch the network.[48] At the time of this writing, the network is still based in Doha and is still being funded by the Qatari government.

After the capture of Bab al-Aziziya, Muammar Gaddafi's main base, in August of 2011, it became clear for the first time that the Qataris were involved on the ground as well, as Qatari special forces were seen on the front lines of the fight.[49] However, Qatar did not formally admit it had sent hundreds of ground troops until late October of 2011.[50]

During the conflict, Qatar helped train the rebels, setting up training camps for them in Benghazi and in the Nafusa Mountains west of Tripoli, as well as bringing Libyan fighters back to Doha for special exercises. Qatar also flew the injured to Doha for medical treatment and provided

46 Azouz, Mohamed. "Qatar Supports Egypt's General Budget with US$500 Million, Increases Investments." *Egypt Independent* 6 Oct. 2011

47 Eakin, Hugh. "The Strange Power of Qatar." *The New York Review of Books* 27 Oct. 2011

48 Watson, Katy. "Libya Conflict: Qatar Tries to Forge a New Global Role." *BBC News* 12 Sept. 2011

49 Roberts, David. "Behind Qatar's Intervention in Libya." *Foreign Affairs* 28 Sept. 2011

50 Black, Ian. "Qatar Admits Sending Hundreds of Troops to Support Libya Rebels." *The Guardian* 26 Oct. 2011

humanitarian aid. Overall, according to BBC, Qatar is estimated to have spent hundreds of millions of dollars so far on Libya.[51]

An October 4, 2011 article published by *The Guardian* cited growing concern among Libyans in the National Transitional Council and Western officials that Qatar had been pursuing its own postwar agenda at the cost of wider efforts to bring political stability to the country. The article said that concern had been mounting that Qatar was bypassing an internationally agreed assistance strategy to Libya to throw its support behind individuals and factions contributing to the continuing political instability.[52]

In the article, an unnamed Western diplomat was quoted as saying, "There is a question now about what foreign players like Qatar are doing in Libya—whether it is being helpful and respectful of Libyan sovereignty. Qatar is not being respectful, and there is a feeling that it is riding roughshod over the issue of the country's sovereignty."[53]

A September 2011 article in *Foreign Affairs* suggested why Qatar might have engaged so stridently: "Above all, it will benefit economically in the post-Gaddafi era after showing so much support to the rebels so quickly. Qatar will likely find itself with a sizeable role in Libya's oil and gas industry and in related sectors such as transportation and facility security. Another benefit of intervention from Doha's perspective has been the lavish praise it has received from key Western allies in London, Paris, and Washington."[54]

At press time, the Qatari flag still flies next to the Libyan flag at checkpoints in that country.

SYRIA

The Syrian uprising, also linked to the Arab Spring, started small but persisted well beyond the capacity of any home-grown rebellion. Syrian President Bashar al-Assad confidently asserted that the government was

51 Buchanan, Michael. "Qatar Flexing Muscle in Changing World." *BBC News* 28 Dec. 2011

52 Beaumont, Peter. "Qatar Accused of Interfering in Libyan Affairs." *The Guardian* 4 Oct. 2011

53 Beaumont, Peter. "Qatar Accused of Interfering in Libyan Affairs." *The Guardian* 4 Oct. 2011

54 Roberts, David. "Behind Qatar's Intervention in Libya." *Foreign Affairs* 28 Sept. 2011

in tune with its people, ready to reform on its own terms, and immune from the turmoil starting to sweep the region.[55]

On March 15, 2011, a few dozen protesters took to the streets of Damascus to call for greater freedoms, setting off one of the most protracted and bloodiest of all the Arab revolts.[56] Soon the uprising was seen throughout the country. Protesters demanded the resignation of the president, the overthrow of his government, and an end to nearly five decades of Ba'ath Party rule. But while other Arab uprisings toppled four leaders in Tunisia, Egypt, Libya and Yemen, Assad has withstood the year-long turmoil, deploying tanks, elite troops and artillery to crush outbreaks across the country.[57]

Indeed, voters approved a new constitution in February 2012 and Assad held parliamentary elections in May. The opposition, which is made up of disparate interests, continue to argue that systematic steps to reform are not enough, and continue to foment violence.

Despite Qatar's good relations with the Assad regime before the Syrian uprising began, it became the first Gulf nation to close its embassy in Damascus[58] and has led the assault against Assad, pressing for his condemnation and boycott in the Arab League while arming and funding the opposition.[59] Sheikh Hamad was also the first to call for arming the Syrian rebels, and has even advocated military intervention to topple Assad.[60]

In March of 2012, Sheikh Hamad told a meeting of Arab foreign ministers in Cairo it was time to send Arab and foreign troops to Syria, according to AFP.

"The time has come to apply the proposal to send Arab and international troops to Syria," Sheikh Hamad said during a meeting of top diplomats. The call came amid Western and Arab-led efforts to pile pressure on Assad's regime. There have been reports that Qatar was sending weapons to arm the Syrian rebels against Assad.

55 Evans, Dominic. "One Year On, Syria's Assad won't Bow to Uprising." *Reuters* 14 Mar. 2012

56 Evans, Dominic. "One Year On, Syria's Assad won't Bow to Uprising." *Reuters* 14 Mar. 2012

57 Evans, Dominic. "One Year On, Syria's Assad won't Bow to Uprising." *Reuters* 14 Mar. 2012

58 Eakin, Hugh. "The Strange Power of Qatar." *The New York Review of Books* 27 Oct. 2011

59 "Deciphering the Qatar Enigma." *Middle East Online* 28 Feb. 2012

60 Smoltczyk, Alexander and Zand, Bernhard. "Tiny Qatar has Big Diplomatic Ambitions." *Der Spiegel* 14 Mar. 2012

In terms of political motivation, Qatar, as a Sunni state wary of the expansion of Shi'a power throughout the region, might appreciate the opportunity to turn Syria away from its current orientation toward Iran.[61]

INFLUENTIAL BUT INEFFECTIVE?

When divided leaders come to Doha for peace talks, their expenses are fully covered by Qatar—including health care. This is a significant draw, especially if quality care is not available in the conflict zones. The *Christian Science Monitor* reported that according to members of past delegations, when negotiating teams arrive, a car service shuttles participants around Doha at the government's expense, and delegations are given a small per diem and free hotel rooms.[62]

However, perks will only get you so far, and results have widely varied, at least in part because of Qatar's relative inexperience as host.

The *Christian Science Monitor* piece reported that two members of the Darfur negotiation team, neither of whom was authorized by their clients to speak on the record, separately described the mediation as disorganized. "Basic standards are not being met here, and the Qataris showed no understanding of why these [missing pieces] were major issues," one recalled. There was no official note-taker, for example, which made implementing the accords almost impossible, as conversations and agreements are remembered differently.

The article goes on to say that in several negotiations, analysts worried that Qatar has been more concerned with getting a deal than ensuring it was a deal that could work on the ground. "Conflict continued well after Yemen signed a Qatari-brokered deal with Houthi separatists there in 2010. Darfur talks have resulted in little change in Sudan's western region. And the recent Palestinian power-sharing deal looks frozen; the two leaders have delayed meeting to form a government since the agreement was signed in early February of 2012."[63]

---

61   Roberts, David. "Behind Qatar's Intervention in Libya." *Foreign Affairs* 28 Sept. 2011

62   Dickinson, Elizabeth. "Qatar Builds Brand as Mediator." *The Christian Science Monitor* 28 Mar. 2012

63   Dickinson, Elizabeth. "Qatar Builds Brand as Mediator." *The Christian Science Monitor* 28 Mar. 2012

Chapter 3: How a Totalitarian Regime Has Taken on the Mantel of Bringing Democracy to the Region

Beyond Qatar's increasingly proactive foreign policy, the country is also engaging in what might be dubbed extensive global PR efforts to bolster its image. This is carried out through a variety of mediums, including, among other things, the country's annual Democracy Forums, the financial support of the Al Jazeera network, and turbo-charged education reform that's attracting the attention of top-notch schools from all over the Western world.

Qatar also frequently plays host to conferences and other events, drawing in people from around the world. Its high level PR efforts paint it as a modern, 21st century, welcoming place to live and work.

But isn't it a paradox for a country with no semblance of democracy to not only be hosting annual Democracy Forums, but also to be sending warplanes to help people fighting for democracy—in other words, the overthrow of leaders tarred as holding too much power—thousands of miles away, as explored in the previous chapter? This chapter explores Qatar's role on the international stage and how the country is using its sovereign fund and surplus gas money to buy influence around the world.

The Guise of Democracy in Qatar

As one of the world's few remaining absolute monarchs, there is little to no democracy in Qatar. The al-Thani Family has ruled Qatar since the mid-1800s, and the emir exercises full executive powers, including appointment of cabinet members.

In 1999, women were granted the right to vote, and the country held the first democratic polls since 1971. The election of Qatar's 29-member municipal council marked the start of a democratization program. The council advises the minister of municipal affairs and agriculture on local issues such as street repair, green space, trash collection, and public works projects for the entire country.

In 2003, a reported 97 percent of voters approved a new constitution in a referendum. The new constitution formally granted women equality and provided for a legislative advisory council comprising 30 elected and 15 appointed members. The constitution also reaffirmed hereditary rule by the emir's male branch of the al-Thani family and reiterated Shari'a (Islamic law) as a primary source of legislation. The emir approves or rejects legislation after consultation with the appointed 35-member Advisory Council and cabinet. There are no elections for national leadership aside from the legislative advisory council proposed in the constitution.

Also noteworthy in 2003: the first woman cabinet minister was elected in Qatar's second municipal council elections.

In 2007 citizens again elected the Municipal Council to four-year terms. Fewer than 50,000 voters were eligible; at least, nearly 50 percent of those participated. The number of eligible voters was so low because, according to the U.S. State Department's 2008 Human Rights Report, approximately 75 percent of citizens could not vote in the 2007 municipal elections as this right was limited to families that were in the country prior to 1930.

All citizens over 21 were permitted to run for seats on the council, regardless of gender. The report says Qatar's law also limits political participation for persons whose citizenship was withdrawn but subsequently restored. These persons are denied the right to candidacy or nomination in any legislative body for a period of 10 years from the date of restoration of their citizenship.

It is important to note that Qatari law also forbids formation of and membership in political parties.

Women's participation in politics has been limited by the influence of traditional attitudes and roles; however, some women served in public office as: minister of health, minister of education; president of the Permanent Election Committee; head of the General Authority for Health, vice president of the Supreme Council for Family Affairs (SCFA) with ministerial rank, head of the General Authority for Museums, and president of Qatar University. Also, one woman served on the Central Municipal Council.

In 2008 Sheikh Hamad postponed elections for the expanded 45-member legislative advisory council and extended the term of the current municipal council for two years.

The ever-present promise of a national election came again in June of 2011, when Sheikh Hamad said there would be a vote for an advisory council in 2013, thereby extending the tenure of the current advisory council. The elections would be Qatar's first legislative elections.

In April of 2011, President Obama met with Sheikh Hamad to praise his help in Libya and leadership "when it comes to democracy in the Middle East."[64] Later that evening, however, President Obama provided a somewhat different, candid opinion. He held a Q-and-A session with donors, with the press present. After the press left, President Obama did not realize he was still speaking on an open mike. Mark Knoller of CBS News recorded his comments.

Of Sheikh Hamad, President Obama said: "He is a big booster, big promoter of democracy all throughout the Middle East. Reform, reform, reform—you're seeing it on Al Jazeera."

He continued: "Now, he himself is not reforming significantly. There's no big move towards democracy in Qatar. But you know part of the reason is that the per capita income of Qatar is $145,000 a year. That will dampen a lot of conflict."[65]

British paper *The Telegraph* reported on the royal family's failure to "introduce any semblance of the democracy it was helping elsewhere to promote, through the Al Jazeera television channel which it owns, and finance with its large-scale backing for the revolution in Libya, has drawn increasing political attention to itself."

The paper also quoted Sheikh Hamad as saying, "We have always preferred that regimes start changes on their own and lead the movement of transformation, instead of seeing people rise up," in an apparent nod to the contradiction.[66]

A Decidedly Un-free Society

Although Qatar was the first Arab country in the Persian Gulf to allow women the right to vote (actually, women and men were granted

---

64   Jackson, David. "Obama: 'No Big Move Toward Democracy in Qatar'." *USA Today* 16 Apr. 2011

65   Jackson, David. "Obama: 'No Big Move Toward Democracy in Qatar'." *USA Today* 16 Apr. 2011

66   Spencer, Richard. "Qatar to Hold National Democratic Elections for the First Time." *The Telegraph* 1 Nov. 2011

suffrage at the same time at the end of the twentieth century) and it is making great strides in education reform, from a Western perspective, the country is lacking in terms of personal freedoms and liberties, from gender equality, to workplace rights, to religious freedoms. Liberties are even fewer and farther between for non-Qatari citizens (which, remember, make up the bulk of the population by a lot—up to 85%). In fact, the watchdog group Freedom House designates Qatar "not free," noting especially the lack of rights for foreign workers.[67] Unsurprisingly, Qatar has also signed very few international human rights conventions.

Women

Thanks in part to Sheikha Mozah, who is a vocal advocate for women's issues through conferences, higher education opportunities, and the creation of a cabinet-level position in the Qatari government dedicated to women's concerns, Qatari women have enjoyed more freedom, including expanded career opportunities. *Gulf News* reported that more than one third of Qatari women work outside their homes.[68]

In a report on women's rights in Qatar, the UN Refugee Agency noted that Qatari law treats women as full and equal persons; however, in practice, "most women living in Qatar are not always treated as equals. The implementation of Islamic laws in Qatar is often discriminatory against women, particularly the laws that govern inheritance and child custody."[69]

Qatar's interpretations of Islamic law deem the testimony of two women to be equal to that of one man. However, the report noted that judicial discretion works to make the courts flexible in applying this rule, and the judge ultimately decides the credibility of witnesses.

The UN Refugee Agency reported that women usually attend court proceedings in legal cases but are typically represented by a male relative or, increasingly, a (male) attorney, although women may represent themselves if they choose. Half of Qatar's judges are non-Qataris who are at-will employees who can be fired and consequently deported at any time, a circumstance that limits their independence.

---

67 Kiefer, Francine. "Qatar: The Small Arab Monarchy with the Loud Democratic Voice." *The Christian Science Monitor* 27 May 2011

68 Toumi, Habib. "Qatari Women Moving Forward with More Rights, Expert Says." *Gulf News* 22 Dec. 2011

69 "Women's Rights in the Middle East and North Africa – Qatar." *Freedom House* 14 Oct. 2005

Only in the year 2000 did Qatari authorities grant the first woman, Haifa al-Bakr, a license to practice law, and in March of 2010, Sheikha Maha Mansour al-Thani was appointed as the first female judge in Qatar.[70]

While the number of women lawyers in Qatar is growing, their proportion within the legal profession and their work remain very limited.

The Qatar embassy boasts of the myriad roles of women in the Qatari workforce, including the fields of education, health, charitable work, law, arts, literature, journalism, aviation, banking, finance, politics and tourism. In reality, however, the types of careers women are able to have are limited by the government. Whether a woman can become a judge or an ambassador is up to the emir, who makes appointments to such posts.

While it is not legally prohibited, few Qatari women or men live alone. Young women would be likely to face familial opposition and possibly male harassment if they tried to live on their own. The report also notes that women have restricted freedom of movement. "While foreign women may obtain a driver's license, Qatari women are required to have the permission of their male guardian (husband, father) to get a license and must prove that their daily life necessitates movement."

Interactions between unrelated men and women are often restricted due to segregation in public areas like workplaces and schools. Restaurants have family rooms for women and families, health clubs have ladies' hours, and banks have women's sections. These practices are enforced only by social norms and tradition, not by religious police, as seen with the mutaween in Saudi Arabia. But posters advertising nightclubs in elite hotels carry the legend, "Qatari ladies not admitted."

Women are not legally required to have a male guardian's permission to travel abroad, but the report notes that few women travel alone, and that men can prevent female relatives from leaving the country by giving their names to immigration officers at departure ports. Employers are able to restrict non-Qatari workers and their ability to travel abroad, a topic that will be explored in chapter six.

Qatari law is based on Shari'a law, and under Islamic law, males rightfully inherit more but ultimately are financially responsible for their female relatives. Females inherit less but retain their share with no obligation to spend any part of it, even on their own needs, such as food or clothing. In accordance with the Shari'a, Qatar's inheritance laws grant

---

70 Elshamy, Anwar. "Dream Comes True for Qatar's First Woman Judge." *Gulf Times* 17 Mar. 2010

wives half the amount of inheritance of male relatives. Non-Muslim wives will not inherit unless previous formal arrangements have been made to provide them with up to one-third of the total inheritance.

Women have the right to own land and property, are allowed to control their income and assets and are legally allowed to enter into business and economic contracts and activities. A number of initiatives have been established in recent years to support the participation of women in this sector, including the Women's Investment Company of Qatar and the Businesswomen's Club, which is a branch of the Qatar Chamber of Commerce and Industry.

Qatari women have equal access to Qatar's free education system. Article 49 of the constitution states, "Education is the right of every citizen. The State shall endeavor to provide free and compulsory public education in accordance with the laws in force." However, the country's educational system is segregated by gender (the University of Qatar has separate campuses for women and men) and opportunities for women within the education system are still limited. The same report on women's rights states that "Due to cultural and societal limits on a woman's ability to travel, females account for only 37 percent of the students who study abroad. Most specialized schools are limited to men; women are not allowed in specialized secondary schools or in the fields of engineering or law at the University of Qatar. Women generally enroll in the theoretical sciences and tend to graduate with similar skills. Consequently, one factor that contributes to women's high unemployment is that there is an oversupply of qualified women competing for positions in fields with little demand."

Workplace and Working Conditions

In Qatar, workers are not permitted to form unions. Protections provided for Qatari citizens, as well as standards of work, are vastly different for noncitizens. A series of restrictive labor laws first implemented in 1962 granted many privileges to citizens, such as preference in hiring.

Unlike what is commonplace in the United States and throughout Europe, there are no laws to protect women from sexual harassment in the workplace and no complaint mechanisms for women to report such cases.

Qatari women do not always receive equal benefits to cover transportation and housing (because these costs are typically covered by their male relatives, as specified in the Shari'a law), but women who are Qatari citizens enjoy some benefits that are unheard of in many Western nations, particularly the U.S.

In general, employers are required to provide at least 50 paid days of maternity leave. The Qatari government, which employs the majority of women in the workforce, allows female employees receive two hours of breaks a day for one year to breast-feed. State-employed Qatari women who have worked for more than four years can receive two-year leaves (the first paid, the second at half pay) on two occasions in their working lives to care for young children. The government also provides working hours that allow most mothers to be home after school if they desire.

Noncitizen Rights

Noncitizens, on the other hand, do not enjoy the same rights. The government distinguishes between citizens and noncitizens in employment, education, housing, and health services. Health care, electricity, water, and education are services that are provided without charge to citizens, but they must be paid for by noncitizens. Noncitizens are permitted to own property in three designated areas. The benefits outlined above that are afforded to Qatari women do not apply to non-Qatari women.

Suspects of nonviolent crimes are entitled to be released on bail, although the U.S. State Department has noted that authorities are more likely to grant citizens bail than noncitizens. Noncitizens charged with minor crimes may be released to their citizen sponsor, although they cannot leave the country until the case is resolved.

It is not easy for a noncitizen to gain citizenship; the Nationality Law allows a maximum of 50 noncitizen residents per year to apply for citizenship after residing in the country 25 consecutive years.

Citizenship derives solely from the father; women do not transmit citizenship to their children, even if they are born in wedlock in the country. A woman must obtain permission from authorities before marrying a foreign national, but she does not lose nationality upon marriage. The State Department reports there were approximately 1,500 "Bidoon" residents (stateless persons with residency ties) in the country, who were unable to register for services such as education and health care.

There is one exception that Qatar is willing to make when granting Qatari citizenship: the case of the Olympic athlete. *Euromoney* reported that the country has "lured several foreign athletes with massive deals to change nationalities and compete for Qatar (although that strategy has brought little Olympic success, yielding just two bronze medals in seven Olympics)."[71]

Qatar's constitution provides for freedom of movement within the country, foreign travel, emigration, and repatriation, but the U.S. State Department notes that the government does not fully respect this right in practice and in some cases has severely restricted foreign travel for noncitizens. All noncitizens require an exit permit from their employers to leave the country, and access to exit permits is dependent on the employer.

Religious Freedoms

As it is with democracy, Qatar is somewhat of a paradox on the topic of religion. Its constitution provides no explicit protection for freedom of religion, and the government continues to prohibit public worship by non-Muslims. Foreign workers and tourists are free to affiliate with other faiths, as long as they are practiced discreetly in private. However, the lack of formal government recognition limits the ability of non-Muslim religious organizations to obtain trade licenses, sponsor clergy, or to open bank accounts in the name of the denomination.

Among non-Muslims, only Christians have requested and been allowed to rent space for public worship. Qatar's Ministry of Justice maintains a registration procedure for Christian marriages performed by registered churches in the country. Adherents of other faiths may privately practice their religion without harassment, but the Government does not permit Hindus, Buddhists, Bah'ais or members of other religions to operate as freely as Christian congregations.

The Catholic, Anglican, and Orthodox churches received de facto official recognition in the latter part of 1999, when the government made a verbal commitment to allow the churches to operate without interference.

Since then, in March 2008 the Roman Catholic Church "Our Lady of the Rosary" was consecrated in Doha. However, no missionaries are allowed and the church has no bells, crosses or other overtly Christian signs on its premises. It is the first official Christian church inaugurated in Qatar and was the first church to be built in Qatar since the seventh century.

Yet, as the monarchy is a frequent host to conferences on democracy (see next section), so too is it a regular host to dialog among religions. Al-

---

71   Ellis, Eric. "David Proctor: The Banker Who Can't Get Out of Qatar." *Euromoney* Jan. 2010

though the country hasn't quite ousted dictators and sent war planes in the name of religion, as of 2011, nine conferences on religious dialog have been held in Doha. Beyond fluffy discussions limited to re-iterance of acceptance, the 2011 conference included discussions about the role of the Internet and social communication media, including Facebook, Twitter and YouTube in promoting dialogue among religions. Specifically, the conference explored how social communication has contributed to the weakening of traditions and customs, the misuse of social networking sites among the religious communities, the ethics of the use of the new technology, and the effects of the use of modern communication technology and its links to developments in liberalization in Arab countries. The conference also included a special session titled "science and religion" that involved participants of a concurrent Islamic science conference.

Further, the Doha International Center for Interfaith Dialogue is a permanent fixture that was established upon a recommendation of the fifth Doha Interfaith Conference in May 2007 in Doha. The center opened in May 2008.

Internet Freedoms and Freedom of Speech

Qatar's constitution provides for freedom of speech and of the press in accordance with the law, but in practice, the government limits these rights, and journalists and publishers regularly self-censor due to political and economic pressures when reporting on government policies or material deemed hostile to Islam, the ruling family, and relations with neighboring states.

The UN Refugee Agency's report on women's rights in Qatar notes that rights of assembly and association in Qatar are limited and that public protest and political demonstrations are rare. All nongovernmental organizations (NGOs) require permission from the state to operate. Political parties, trade groups, women's groups, and human rights groups have been refused licenses.

Although publicly embracing social media and other Internet technology, the U.S. State Department reports that Qatar's government has restricted the peaceful expression of views via the Internet and censored the Internet for political, religious, and pornographic content through a proxy server, which monitored and blocked Web sites, e-mail, and chat rooms through the state-owned Internet service provider. The report notes the example of the popular blog "Ikhbareya," which at times published articles critical of the government. The government blocked access to the site. Any user who believed a site was mistakenly censored could submit the Web address to have the site reviewed for suitability, but there were no reports that any Web sites were unblocked based on this procedure.

Finally, while Qatari laws prohibiting same-sex relations are far from the topic of this book, their existence paints a broader picture about the state of human rights in Qatar as compared to other countries. Oddly, the law prohibits same-sex relations between men but is silent concerning same-sex relations between women. Under the criminal law, a man convicted of having sexual relations with another man or boy younger than 16 years old is subject to a sentence of life in prison. A man convicted of having sexual relations with another man older than 16 years old is subject to a sentence of seven years in prison under section 285 of the criminal law.

Annual Democracy Forums Hosted by a Totalitarian Regime

As referenced in the section on religious freedoms, there is a bit of a paradox here: Qatar, a totalitarian regime with little semblance of democracy, hosts regular democracy forums, part of the PR machine working to portray Qatar as a benevolent world power. On this endeavor, the country teamed up with the prestigious American think tank the Brookings Institution and the Saban Center for Middle East Policy.

The 12th annual forum on Democracy, Development and Free Trade was held in 2012. Panelists and speakers come from all over the world. Recent discussions included the Arab Spring, the political future of the Middle East, economic causes of discontent, trade, water security, enriching regional economies through sports, and media, among other topics.

Beyond the Democracy Forums, Qatar is a frequent host to peace talks, and even beyond the state-sponsored talks, Qatar is looking to set up a Middle East Development Bank to support Arab countries as they undergo political upheavals; that is, to co-opt them and enlarge Qatar's sphere of influence.[72] The bank would be modeled on the European Bank of Reconstruction and Development that proved so crucial in helping

---

72 Kiefer, Francine. "Qatar: The Small Arab Monarchy with the Loud Democratic Voice." *The Christian Science Monitor* 27 May 2011

Central and Eastern Europe integrate with Western Europe after the fall of the Berlin Wall.[73]

Qatar is also a frequent host to conferences like the Doha Round of the WTO. The talks are nicknamed the Doha Round due to fact that they were launched in Doha, even though they mainly took place in Geneva. A related term, the Doha Development Agenda, emphasizes that development is a main objective and underscores that negotiations are one half of the work program—the other half deals with problems that developing countries face in the implementation of the present agreements.

Using Al Jazeera as the Mouthpiece of the Government

Al Jazeera is a 24-hour Arabic-language satellite television news network viewable throughout the Middle East and most of the world. The station filled a void in that it was the first news network broadcast in Arabic specifically for the Arab world, in a style similar to CNN or BBC. One of its key strengths was that it offered an alternative to broadcasters controlled by national governments, whose coverage invariably reflected narrow regime interests rather than a popular understanding of events.[74]

The station first went on the air on November 1, 1996, after Sheikh Hamad hired a league of out-of-work Arab journalists who had lost their jobs with the BBC and gave them a mandate to make his rival autocrats uncomfortable (boosting his political juice throughout the region in the process).[75]

Al Jazeera quickly became popular throughout the Middle East, and with the onslaught of post-9/11 bin Laden coverage, the station also became commonly known throughout the Western world through clips played on English-speaking networks. Suddenly Al Jazeera was, if not a worldwide phenomenon, at least a globally-recognized name.

However, despite the easy branding of Al Jazeera as the CNN of the Arab world, there is one key difference: the network is owned by the state of Qatar through the Qatar Media Corporation.

Although Al Jazeera executives and newscasters say they work independently of Sheikh Hamad, when the network was launched, he provided a loan of QAR 500 million ($137 million) to sustain Al Jazeera through its first five years. The seed money was one of the largest single

---

73 Kiefer, Francine. "Qatar: The Small Arab Monarchy with the Loud Democratic Voice." *The Christian Science Monitor* 27 May 2011

74 Noe, Nicholas and Raad, Walid. "Al-Jazeera Gets Rap as Qatar Mouthpiece." *Bloomberg* 9 Apr. 2012

75 Pintak, Lawrence. "The Al Jazeera Revolution." *Foreign Policy* 2 Feb. 2011

gifts ever granted to a media corporation and it went a long way in promoting Qatar as a stable, business-friendly environment.[76] The station was supposed to become self sufficient within that timeframe, but today, Qatar maintains a large stake in Al Jazeera and uses the network to push its own political agendas. It's quickly gaining a reputation as Qatar's mouthpiece, and in a report on Qatar, the U.S. State Department noted that Qatar's government exercised editorial and programmatic control of the channel through funding and selection of the station's management.

It could be argued that Al Jazeera is Sheikh Hamad's most important tool (perhaps second only to his billions).

According to the Al Jazeera Network's own statistics, the channel has an estimated audience of over 50 million viewers, and that number continues to grow as the network expands its reach. With the launch of the English-language in 2006, ten years after the network launched in Arabic, its reach became even bigger. Interestingly, Al Jazeera English's staff of about 140 was hired away from CNN, NBC, CBS, and other U.S. stations[77], although the network is still not widely carried in the U.S. Al Jazeera also now has a station devoted solely to the Balkans, as well as new programming for Latin America and Africa.[78]

Despite the network's popularity and easy name recognition, it has faced somewhat of a backlash of late.

By 2002, nearly every country in the Arab League had formally protested unfavorable coverage on Al Jazeera[79], and the WikiLeaks cables brought a whole new set of allegations against Qatar and its intentions with the network. In 2010 *The Guardian* reported that U.S. embassy cables released by WikiLeaks claim Qatar is using Al-Jazeera as a bargaining chip in foreign policy negotiations by adapting its coverage to suit other foreign leaders and offering to cease critical transmissions in exchange for major concessions.[80]

76 Dietz, David. "How Qatar Rose to Become a Leading Player in Middle East Politics." *Policymic* Jan. 2012

77 McKelvey, Tara. "In Arabic in English in D.C." *The American Prospect* 17 Dec. 2006

78 Smoltczyk, Alexander and Zand, Bernhard. "Tiny Qatar has Big Diplomatic Ambitions." *Der Spiegel* 14 Mar. 2012

79 Eakin, Hugh. "The Strange Power of Qatar." *The New York Review of Books* 27 Oct. 2011

80 Booth, Robert. "WikiLeaks Cables Claim al-Jazeera Changed Coverage to Suit Qatari Foreign Policy." *The Guardian* 5 Dec. 2010

The Arab Spring served to further tarnish Al Jazeera's image and pro-vide easy ammunition to those who allege the network's coverage is bi-ased and selective.

While the network received significant praise for its coverage of the Egyptian uprisings and beginning of the Arab Spring, it has been accused of inconsistent coverage; while Egypt, Libya and Yemen's revolts were widely covered, demonstrations in nearby Bahrain were noticeably un-derreported. Coincidentally, Qatar backed Saudi troops in Bahrain to put down democratic protesters there (Qatar says it had to fulfill its alliance obligations[81]).

Further, the *New York Times* reported that while a senior Al Jazeera journalist there said no order was given, the network's reporting on Syria changed sharply in April. "We could feel the change in atmosphere," the journalist said.[82]

Doha Debates

Beyond Al Jazeera, Qatar has found an additional way to reach inter-national masses through its Doha Debates, which have been broadcast on BBC World News since January 2005. The debates are held in Qatar once a month and are billed as a forum for free speech in the Arab world. Internationally controversial and even taboo topics, such as whether de-mocracy is more important than wealth; whether France is right to ban the face veil; government accountability; political Islam; and the status of women in the Arab world, are covered.

The Doha Debates are an initiative of the Qatar Foundation for Edu-cation, Science and Community Development, which was founded in 1995 and chaired by Sheikha Mozah. The BBC purchases a license from Qatar Foundation, which gives it first broadcast rights for the debates.

Although the Debates are financed by the Qatar Foundation, it is stressed that no government, official body or broadcaster has any control over what is said at the sessions or who is invited, and this particular broadcast medium hasn't seemed to face much controversy or opposition.

---

81 Kiefer, Francine. "Qatar: The Small Arab Monarchy with the Loud Democratic Voice." *The Christian Science Monitor* 27 May 2011
82 Shadid, Anthony. "Qatar Wields an Outsize Influence in Arab Politics." *The New York Times* 14 Nov. 2011

SHAPING THE PERCEPTION OF YOUTH—IN QATAR AND ELSEWHERE

One way a totalitarian regime is able to keep the peace at home, amid other nations rising in the Arab Spring, is to make life exceedingly easy for its youth, and that is a tactic Qatar obviously employs.

The native population may have no political freedom, but it certainly enjoys economic freedom, ensured by very generous stipends the state provides them, along with free education, healthcare, housing and jobs. All Qataris are entitled to free education, from pre-school to post graduate education. The government, Qatar Petroleum, Q-Tel or one of the major Qatari banks will sponsor the education of any Qatari in Qatar or abroad.

Qataris receive preferential treatment in hiring, and through the Qatarization Act, all companies in Qatar have to maintain a minimum number of Qatari employees. The bulk of Qataris choose to work in the government because of the lax work environment and flexible hours. The security service is predominantly or entirely Qatari.

Healthcare is available to residents of Qatar, including expatriates. However, Qataris enjoy the added benefit of free healthcare anywhere in the world. They can choose to travel overseas if they need additional treatment that is not available in Qatar. All Qataris qualify for a free plot of land when they get married, and through the Qatari Development Bank, receive subsidized no interest loans to build a house. They also receive a financial gift from the government when they get married and have a child. From time to time, the Emir will issue a directive absolving Qataris of their mortgages, and to an extent, certain bank loans. Qataris also enjoy favorable treatment from local banks, and banks offer Qataris the opportunity to borrow up 200 times their monthly salary.

The Arab Youth Survey is conducted annually among eighteen- to twenty-four-year-olds in ten Arab countries by PR firm Burson-Marstell-er to find out what the largest demographic of the Middle Eastern region is really thinking. In an article titled "The Strange Power of Qatar," *New York Book Review* writer Hugh Eakin noted that the most recent Arab Youth Survey found that "just one third of Qatari respondents—the lowest of any country polled—ranked democracy as 'very important,' compared to nearly three fourths in the neighboring emirate of Abu Dhabi. The same survey also found that 88 percent of young Qataris thought their country was 'going in the right direction.'"[83]

---

83 Eakin, Hugh. "The Strange Power of Qatar." *The New York Review of Books* 27 Oct. 2011

The article goes on to suggest that by taking the lead in Arab support for the Libyan rebels, Sheikh Hamad has not merely put his country on the side of revolutionaries (and, in its direct support for various individual rebel leaders, maximized its chances of picking an ultimate winner); it has also allowed Qatar and other Gulf states that have followed suit to show they are responsible members (read: aligned with Western interests) of the international community, while deflecting attention from the Gulf itself.[84]

Sheikh Hamad and Sheikha Mozah have spearheaded liberal social reforms that have not always been popular with more conservative tribal elders.[85] Education reform, in particular, is a popular topic in Qatar these days, and has been since Sheikh Hamad put his second wife, Sheikha Mozah, in charge of it. The same article by Eakin reports that over the past decade, Qatar hired the American thinktank RAND to revamp its K–12 education system along contemporary Western lines. Through the Qatar Foundation, the country has built a 2,500-acre "Education City" for local outposts of the Weill Cornell Medical College, Georgetown's School of Foreign Service, Northwestern's Medill School of Journalism, Texas A&M's School of Engineering, and other Western institutions.[86] See the appendix for more information on Western companies' presences in Qatar.

The amount of social support is practically unheard of from any Western viewpoint; health care, electricity, water, and education are provided without charge to citizens. The country's health-care system covers a range of issues, including mental and dental care and a complete maternity care program.

Indeed, if everything is paid for and everyone (well, every citizen, anyway) has enough money to comfortably live out the rest of his or her life, what's the point of protesting against the monarch?

PROMOTING DEMOCRACY? OR DISILLUSIONED DREAMS OF CONTROLLING THE WORLD?

But is that democracy? Or is it more like a disillusioned dream of controlling the world? Germany's *Der Spiegel* reported that there is specu-

---

84 Eakin, Hugh. "The Strange Power of Qatar." *The New York Review of Books* 27 Oct. 2011

85 Spencer, Richard. "Qatar to Hold National Democratic Elections for the First Time." *The Telegraph* 1 Nov. 2011

86 Eakin, Hugh. "The Strange Power of Qatar." *The New York Review of Books* 27 Oct. 2011

lation that Sheikh Hamad has a religious agenda, namely to strengthen Sunni Islam, the country's dominant religion. The same article also referenced those who believe that tiny Qatar has sinister designs to "conquer the world", as the French newspaper *Le Monde* puts it.[87]

Sheikh Hamad's recent international purchases and investments include the following:

1. In Germany, Qatar's sovereign wealth fund, the Qatar Investment Authority, owns 17 percent of the carmaker Volkswagen, 10 percent of Porsche and 9 percent of the construction giant Hochtief.[88]

2. Qatar is seeking to acquire a stake in the aerospace corporation EADS in France, where it already owns shares in the Suez energy group, Dexia Bank and the Lagardère publishing group. The emir has also acquired the football club Paris Saint-Germain.[89]

3. Qatar set up a 50 million euro fund in December 2011 to invest in Muslim suburbs in French cities.[90]

4. In Britain, Qatar owns Harrods (since 2010) and large property stakes. The Qatar Foundation has supported a Doha branch of Bloomsbury, the British publishing house.[91] BBC even aired a story titled, "Why is Qatar buying up London landmarks?"[92]

5. In 2007, Qatar and Dubai became the two biggest shareholders of the London Stock Exchange, the world's third largest stock exchange.

6. In 2012, Qatar's investment fund purchased Italy's Costa Smeralda resort area on the island of Sardinia.[93]

87 Smoltczyk, Alexander and Zand, Bernhard. "Tiny Qatar has Big Diplomatic Ambitions." *Der Spiegel* 14 Mar. 2012

88 Smoltczyk, Alexander and Zand, Bernhard. "Tiny Qatar has Big Diplomatic Ambitions." *Der Spiegel* 14 Mar. 2012

89 Irish, John. "France's Le Pen Attacks Qatar, Fears Islamist Threat." *Reuters* 13 Jan. 2012

90 Irish, John. "France's Le Pen Attacks Qatar, Fears Islamist Threat." *Reuters* 13 Jan. 2012

91 Eakin, Hugh. "The Strange Power of Qatar." *The New York Review of Books* 27 Oct. 2011

92 "Why is Qatar Buying Up London Landmarks?" *BBC* 1 May 2011

93 Totaro, Lorenzo. "Qatar Fund Buys Italy's Costa Smeralda Resort, Sheikh Hamad Says." *Bloomberg* 16 Apr. 2012

7. Further, the emirate is buying agricultural land and investing in banks, tourism and real estate from Ukraine to Pakistan to Thailand.[94]

This isn't a comprehensive list; it's just a short sampling of Qatar's financial action outside of the Middle East. Not only must neighboring Arab countries respect Qatar for sharing a common heritage, language and religion, but also for Qatar's significant investments in their countries. A *PolicyMic* article reported that the majority state-owned Qatar Investment Authority has postponed much of the six billion dollars of investments tied up in Syria. Instead, Jordan has become the beneficiary of those investments. Similarly, countries such as Palestine, Lebanon, and Morocco have taken advantage of hundreds of millions of dollars from Qatari financial subsidiaries and are thus dependent on and beholden to Qatar.[95]

Conquer the world? Seems a bit extreme, but maybe not.

---

94 Smoltczyk, Alexander and Zand, Bernhard. "Tiny Qatar has Big Diplomatic Ambitions." *Der Spiegel* 14 Mar. 2012

95 Dietz, David. "How Qatar Rose to Become a Leading Player in Middle East Politics." *Policymic* Jan. 2012

CHAPTER 4: A SPONSORSHIP SYSTEM AKIN TO SLAVERY

Many are not familiar with the "kafala" system used throughout the Gulf region. The word "kafala" translates to "sponsorship," and throughout the Gulf, this system requires all foreign workers to have an in-country sponsor who is responsible for their visa and legal status.

In theory, the kafala system was put into place as a way to monitor the number of foreigners working in Gulf Arab countries, as many of those countries rely on cheap foreign labor to fill the roles nationals will not do themselves. There is a tremendous demand for labor due to the rapid expansion seen throughout the Gulf—Qatar is not alone in its stunning development.

Most of the foreign labor throughout the Gulf is recruited from countries from the Indian subcontinent. An entire book could be devoted to the struggles faced by that population in Qatar, but for the purposes of this book, it is important to note that many Westerners taking white-collar, prestigious jobs have been hurt by this system as well. That will be covered extensively in the appendix.

The kafala system dates back centuries and has cultural and historical roots in the Arab world. It originated with the Bedouin custom of temporarily granting strangers protection and even affiliation into the tribe for specific purposes. For instance, if a stranger were traveling across the desert and happened to wander onto a family's camp, it would be customary to take him in, feed him and his animals, and allow him to stay as long as he wished.

The modern-day kafala system, however, has morphed into something else entirely and is not nearly as welcoming or forgiving as the Bedouin custom sounds.

Human rights groups frequently criticize the system for placing workers at the mercy of their employers. It has become commonplace for employers to confiscate passports (despite recent laws prohibiting the practice), and employers sometimes use possession of travel documents to extort a large fee before the workers can leave the country.[96]

In fact, many writers have called the kafala system "modern day slavery," as many workers, especially construction and domestic migrant laborers, are held against their will, unable to leave and unable to seek employment elsewhere in the country.

I was no different, and while trapped in Qatar, I began to think of myself as an economic hostage or slave.

However, the situation may be beginning to change ever so slightly throughout the Gulf, albeit slowly. Over the past few years, major international public outcry has essentially prompted the Gulf countries to abolish the kafala system, or at the very least, pretend that they are considering abolishing it.

The International Labor Organization had set a June 2008 deadline for the six member countries of the Gulf Cooperation Council (GCC) to abolish the system (the GCC is made up of Bahrain, Kuwait, Oman, Qatar, Saudi Arabia and United Arab Emirates). The deadline came and went.

Following that nonevent, several non-governmental organizations in Asian countries came together to urge Gulf States to scrap their sponsorship system, with little success.

Then finally, in 2009, Bahrain was the first to announce it would do away with its sponsorship system for foreign workers. As reported by BBC, Bahraini Labor Minister Majeedal-Alawi said the main change in the regulations would mean foreign workers would now be directly sponsored by the Labor Authority and would not depend on their employers.[97] In the same article, BBC reported that al-Alawi even went as far as to liken the kafala system to slavery.

News analysis following Bahrain's move indicated that other Gulf countries would be unlikely to also drop or amend the system, and yet, shortly after, the United Arab Emirates announced it planned to ease

96 Harmassi, Mohammed. "Bahrain to End 'Slavery' System." *BBC* 6 May 2009
97 Harmassi, Mohammed. "Bahrain to End 'Slavery' System." *BBC* 6 May 2009

restrictions and permit laborers to look for other jobs if their employer delays wages by more than two months. The UAE also announced that visas could be extended for foreigners who are let go so that they might find other work in the country. It was a small step.

In 2010, the U.S. State Department issued a 373-page report that urged GCC states to do away with the sponsorship system. The report said that employers in the Gulf States exploit the kafala system to abuse workers. It also named Saudi Arabia and Kuwait as the region's worst offenders.

Shortly after, Kuwait's Minister of Labor and Social Affairs, Mohammed al-Afasi, announced that the government would move towards abolishing the kafala system. Al-Afasi described the move as a "gift" to foreign workers on the 10th anniversary of Kuwait's liberation during the first Gulf War. However, although al-Afasi gave February 2011 as the timeframe for abolishing the sponsorship system in, according to a 2012 Human Rights Watch World Report, the government made no major sponsorship reforms during the year.

The announcement itself was big news, at least, but the UAE did not follow Kuwait's announcement either, although some expected it might do so. Two weeks after Kuwait announced plans to scrap its kafala system, the UAE's labor minister said the UAE would not, despite the Human Rights Watch's urging it to. Oman has also not amended its system.

Saudi Arabia has also received significant bad publicity about its kafala system, but the country has been slow to make any real changes. In 2012, Saudi Arabia's Labor Ministry completed a study on the prospects of canceling the individual kafala system, replacing it with recruitment companies. *Arab News* reported that the move may lead to the nullification of sponsorship system altogether at a later stage.

The study, which took five years to complete, proposed the formation of a commission under the Labor Ministry to look into foreign labor issues and put an end to the traditional sponsorship system. The commission was to be based in Riyadh with branches in other major cities. The study also advised the government not to hold passports of foreign workers and to cancel the condition of obtaining sponsor's approval for a worker to bring his family to the Kingdom.

BEYOND THE GCC: AN IN-DEPTH LOOK AT THE KAFALA SYSTEM

In Qatar, workers receive an entry visa and residence permit only if a Qatari citizen, institution or company employs them, and this generally must be arranged prior to the worker's entry to Qatar. Foreign workers may enter the country on a tourist visa, but a sponsor is needed to convert a visitor's visa to a work visa and thereafter the worker must have the sponsor's permission to depart the country. In order to convert a visitor's visa to a work visa, the individual must find a job and have his prospective employer submit paperwork to the Ministry of Interior requesting the transfer of visa status. These requests usually are rejected, forcing the individual to travel out of Qatar and return immediately under the work visa.

The law requires the employer to assume full economic and legal responsibility for the employee during the contract period. In addition, the worker can only work for the sponsor. It is possible to change jobs and transfer sponsorship to a new employer only after the foreigner has worked at the sponsoring company for at least two years and has been granted a no objection certificate (frequently called NOCs). In essence, the worker is entirely dependent on the sponsor to enter the country, remain in the country, and of course, as I became well aware, leave the country.

The law goes beyond visas, too; foreign workers need their sponsor's permission to open a bank account, obtain an alcohol permit, or carry out other numerous other activities that are considered basic rights elsewhere. If a worker leaves the job, he can be blocked from returning to Qatar for two years.

If an employee sues the sponsor for violating labor practices, there is no form of unemployment protection while the case is pending in the legal system. And even if the worker wins the case, the usual result is for the sponsor contract to be terminated, meaning that the worker has to leave the country. Essentially, the worker is just suing for his right to leave and will likely never see any lost wages.

The 2012 Human Rights Watch report on Qatar noted that the country has some of the "most restrictive sponsorship laws in the Persian Gulf region." Qatar, however, has given little indication that the outdated system will be revised or abolished, despite the attention Qatar (and its labor laws) will receive as the country gears up for the 2022 World Cup. The country has announced it intends to drop the sponsorship system for expatriates, replacing it with a contract which will be binding on both the employer and the employee. However, no time-frame for the introduction of the "contract" system has been given.

Perhaps surprisingly, Qatar has a National Committee for Human Rights. It is made up of representatives from civil society and various government ministries. Early in 2011, the committee called for discussion of the sponsorship law and amendments that reflect changes in society.

Al-Shorfa reported that Dr. Kaltham al-Ghanim, head of the committee's researchers, said the sponsorship system has "positive aspects that help control migration, but it also has negative aspects such as employers not paying wages on time, seizure of workers' passports and the reluctance to transfer sponsorship."[98]

He was also quoted as saying, "There are differences in the manner of dealing with this law. Employers believe the law guarantees them their rights and prevents a heavy influx of labor into the country."

According to the popular blog "Qatar Visitor," the sponsorship system in Qatar has been weakened somewhat by a series of new laws introduced in 2009. For example, some individuals working in the financial sector do not require sponsorship, and now many people can obtain multiple exit visas, meaning they do not need to obtain specific permission each time they want to leave the country.

The blog also reported that in 2009 Sheikh Hamad himself spoke out against the sponsorship system, arguing that "the sponsorship law was holding back the development of the country."

And yet, the country backpedaled a bit in March of 2011. *Gulf News* reported that month that Qatar had delayed all studies related to sponsorship amendments, waiting to first see the results in Kuwait and Bahrain. The article said, "Labor Ministry undersecretary Hussein al-Mulla said that Qatar would try to avoid the 'negative aspects' resulting from the move in the two neighboring countries. He said a strategy was underway to encourage the nationals to be involved in the labor market. The strategy, which runs until 2016, includes measures to improve the living conditions of foreign workers and to establish a database."[99]

Further, several newspaper articles have reported that Qatari nationals want stricter sponsorship rules.

Gulf News reported on a survey that was part of a series of studies conducted on major local social and economic issues by Qatar University's Social and Economic Research Institute. In the survey, 47 percent

98   El Ghanem, Nasser. "Qatar Considers Review of Sponsorship Law." *Al-Shorfa* 11 Jan. 2011

99   "Sponsorship System Studies 'Delayed'." *Gulf Times* 13 Mar. 2011

of the Qatari respondents said they would like the kafala system to be tightened.[100]

The survey, called "The Omnibus: A Survey of Life in Qatar," featured a random sample of 2,139 people, including 768 expatriate white-collar workers and 682 blue-collar workers. It was conducted between May 18 and June 20, 2010 through face-to-face data collection. Expatriate domestic hands were not covered.[101]

Ninety-five percent of Qataris felt that expatriates increased traffic congestion and 75 percent said they put a strain on the country's health services; 77 percent of the Qatari respondents said they believe there are too many expatriates and migrant workers in the country, and 62 percent said they think the number of labor migrants allowed in the country each year should be decreased. Another 58 percent felt foreign workers weaken the country and take away its resources.

Despite the somewhat apparent animosity towards foreign workers, the survey also indicated that respondents were aware that their country's development is due in large part to foreign workers: 89 percent of respondents said they believe that the hard work and talents of foreign workers have contributed to the development of Qatar.

In addition to general citizen support of the sponsorship law, Qatar's business community of course staunchly supports it.

The Peninsula, an English-language local paper, reported that the private sector admits the sponsorship and exit permit systems have been retained in Qatar's 2009 sponsorship law because of its own influence. The Qatar Chamber of Commerce and Industry (QCCI), the representative body of the private sector, says it backs the exit permit and sponsorship regulations to the hilt and wants these rules to continue.[102]

To be even more specific about Qatar in particular, let's take a look at what is required to enter Qatar on a work visa (which is somewhat of a human rights violation in itself, in terms of invasion of privacy).

In order to procure the required permits, the sponsoring company must hire a public relation officer (PRO) eligible to submit applications and collect permits issued by the immigration authorities. The PRO

---

100 Toumi, Habib. "Qatari Nationals Want Stricter Sponsorship Rules." *Gulf News* 5 Jan. 2011

101 Toumi, Habib. "Qatari Nationals Want Stricter Sponsorship Rules." *Gulf News* 5 Jan. 2011

102 "QCCI Wants Sponsorship, Exit Permits to Continue." *The Peninsula* 11 Oct. 2010

must have supporting documents to prove his relation with the company in the Immigration Department.

The standard immigration procedure to obtain work legally and stay in Qatar takes place in several stages and has pretty stringent requirements:

1. Entry Permit: The employment visa (entry permit) is valid for six months and allows entry into Qatar to take up employment. A foreigner may start working after arrival, but within three months of entry, the employer must complete the formalities in order for the foreigner to receive a residence permit.

2. Medical Check: In order to apply for a residence permit, a health check is needed, including blood tests and chest x-ray. A medical test appointment is arranged by the company PRO after arrival. If the sponsored employee is medically unfit, the immigration office may request immediate repatriation. Note that the blood test performed in the medical check screens for HIV, and no one with HIV is permitted to enter Qatar.

3. Fingerprinting: Fingerprints are taken as a requirement for residence permit application. Once medical results are published online, the PRO will arrange the necessary appointment.

4. Residence Permit and ID card: Applications for residence permits and ID cards are made simultaneously by the PRO through the Immigration Department.

5. A police clearance (certificate of good conduct) may also be required prior to entry.

A report on Qatar by the U.S. State Department noted that a 2009 Sponsorship Law outlawed the practice of employers withholding workers' passports but retained the provision requiring workers to obtain exit permits from their employers before leaving the country.

The report says, "In practice some employers continued to retain workers' passports. Although the law provides an administrative procedure for obtaining an exit permit without an employer's approval, the process was burdensome. Foreign embassies reported that the process was ineffective, and they continued to be requested to mediate disputes concerning exit permits between foreign workers and their sponsors."

The report went on to say that the Sponsorship Law that took effect in March 2009 gives the Ministry of Interior the power to transfer a worker's sponsorship temporarily to another employer if there is a legal dispute between the worker and the original employer. However, some employers temporarily withheld consent to an exit permit and thereby were able to force foreign employees to work for longer periods than they wished.

FILING COMPLAINTS AND DEMONSTRATING, DESPITE A CULTURE
OF SILENCE

According to Qatari labor law, complaints can be filed with the Labor Department, but few such cases make it very far. Human rights advocacy groups such as Human Rights Watch and Amnesty International do not have a strong presence within the country, and there is a culture of silence and fear in reporting abuses—although an inquiring tourist (a rare breed) will find that just about every taxi driver, pool attendant and hotel employee is in a state of controlled rage, or despair.

Despite the culture of silence, in the first quarter of 2010 more than 4,000 workers in Qatar lodged complaints with the Labor Ministry. Of the complaints, 3,875 cases were about employers delaying salaries. Other common problems related to the denial of flight tickets, end-of-service benefits and vacation allowance. According to the report, 64.3 percent of the complaints received during the first quarter were settled. Another 20.2 percent were closed either because the complaint was not one that the Labor Ministry could deal with or the parties did not follow up on the complaints. Fewer than seven percent of cases were sent to court, while another seven percent were under consideration. Construction workers formed the largest segment of complainants, with 63.4 percent, and the wholesale and retail sectors comprised 13.8 percent. Workers in other sectors accounted for 22.8 percent.[103]

In a report on Qatar, the U.S. State Department said that one foreign embassy reported that it received approximately 3,000 complaints from its citizens working in Qatar during one year. Most of the complaints were related to nonpayment of salaries, failure to pay overtime, alteration in promised job and salary scale, alteration in contact terms after arrival, overload of work, compelling the company's workers to serve as domestic help, delayed stamping of resident permits, poor access to health care facilities, maltreatment, and physical abuse.

---

103 Sambidge, Andy. "Salary Delay is No 1 Worker Complaint in Qatar in Q1." *Arabian Business* 23 Jun. 2010

The report went on to say that the 2009 changes in the sponsorship law accounted for a steep drop in the number of complaints against sponsors for retaining employees' passports (the fine for withholding an employee passport is 10,000 riyals, approximately $2,747). Another foreign embassy received between 50 and 60 complaints of abuse a day, including sexual harassment, delay and nonpayment of salaries, forced labor, contract switching, passport retention, poor accommodations, nonrepatriation, termination and deportation without cause, physical torture or torment, overwork, imprisonment, and mistreatment.

As time goes on without significant reform throughout most of the GCC on this issue, in some cases tensions have escalated and workers have attempted to revolt.

One such outburst involved Filipino migrant workers in Saudi Arabia, who, according to the *Education for Development* magazine, have a long history of waging campaigns for the immediate repatriation of stranded workers. The first was in 1997 when up to 2,000 stranded workers from Riyadh were successfully sent home as a result of the campaign, which was coordinated in Saudi Arabia, Hong Kong and the Philippines.[104]

According to the same report, actions by migrant workers in the UAE protesting against contract substitution and unfair provisions in the contract are not tolerated by the Ministry of Labor. The report says that "UAE authorities have been alarmed by recent actions by migrant workers and have stated that they will only recognize three legal reasons for protest, i.e., unpaid wages, poor living conditions and lack of safety procedures. Other than these three, the Ministry of Labor stated migrant workers would be violating the law and would jeopardize their stay in the country if they protested against other issues. According to the Ministry, the workers had to respect the contract that they signed, even if it is a common practice for said agreements to be substituted and violated."[105]

Unfortunately press censorship curbs publicity of such actions, and not much has been heard about other such uprisings.

---

104 "Sponsorship System and its Effects on Expatriate Workers in the Gulf Cooperation Council (GCC) Countries." *Education for Development Magazine* 28 Dec. 2009

105 "Sponsorship System and its Effects on Expatriate Workers in the Gulf Cooperation Council (GCC) Countries." *Education for Development Magazine* 28 Dec. 2009

A Country where the Vast Majority of the Population Has No Rights

With the highest ratio of migrants to citizens in the world, the vast majority of those living in Qatar have extremely limited human rights. Of the almost 1.2 million documented migrant workers currently employed in Qatar, it is difficult to estimate the full extent of employee mistreatment.

Migrant workers flock to Qatar in order to provide for their families back home. They are in no position to ask detailed questions, and it's hard to imagine that many of them fully understand the laws. Countless stories of workers trapped in terrible working environments, with hardly any rights and no way to leave, show that Qatar's kafala system is indeed akin to modern day slavery. Qatar is the world's fastest growing country, yet it is being built on the backs of economic slaves.

Qatar is working hard to burnish its image around the world as a quickly advancing nation, yet its labor laws are not based on international standards. There is a disconnect there that is hard to reconcile with the modern, liberal image Qatar is trying to project. No doubt, it's an odd system for a country that outwardly champions the cause of freedom. Unfortunately, there is no comprehensive Human Rights Code protection in Qatar, as exists in most Western nations. So it appears that without a surge of domestic or international pressure, there is very little the Qatari government will do to address this crisis.

Chapter 5: The Cost of Doing Business in Qatar

Now that we have painted a basic picture of Qatar, I will resume the story of my own experience—how I became an economic hostage. When I moved to Doha in 2007, the city was bustling. Qatar's economy was booming. It had launched an ambitious investment program in tapping and exporting its vast reserves of liquefied natural gas—the third largest proven reserves in the world. Its small population of approximately 250,000 native Qataris could not support the economic growth and newfound wealth, and foreigners were flocking in to fill many of the new jobs being created at every level of the country's gas-fueled economy.

You felt a sense of dynamic excitement in the air. Airline reservations to Qatar were hard to come by, and hotels were frequently booked to full capacity. Hotel lobbies everywhere became centers for wheeling and dealing. No matter where you went, you could see white-robed Qataris holding court, seated on divans and upholstered armchairs in cool marble salons, negotiating with the multitude of foreigners trying to get a piece of the Qatari economic pie.

There was an optimistic sense that Qatar's gold rush offered an economic bonanza to all those who ventured to the country. And the influx of foreign workers benefitted the Qatari population, too; Qatari law mandates all non-Qataris coming to do business give a local partner 51% of any venture, so Qataris were making millions off the ingenuity, sweat and toil of these foreigners. Their only investments were their names and citizenship.

By 2008, gas production reached over 80,000,000 cubic meters annually—equivalent to 500,000 barrels of oil. That same year, Qatar was able to make it through the great financial crash relatively unscathed—at least, that's how it looked—by dipping into its sovereign wealth fund. (By 2011, its stock market was said to be at 17% of its former value.) And so Qatar's economy continued to grow, fueled solely by an increase in gas and its downstream production, while the rest of the world was feeling the first pangs of the recession.

Qatar's PR machine was keen on showing that Qatar was untouched by the financial meltdown of 2008. However, those of us living in Qatar witnessed the effects on the country's economy. Overnight, Doha had emptied. The vibrancy was gone and the excitement dissipated. The gas sector continued to grow, however, and investment was strong, which led to the growth that Qatar would boast to the world. Meanwhile, the U.S. was accelerating its military build-up, though numbers are hard to come by and their presence is not obvious within the city of Doha.

While the world's economies contracted, Qatar experienced 25.4% growth in 2008 and 9.6% in 2009. In 2010, Qatar had the world's highest economic growth rate. However, these figures are deceptive, because the growth was in just one sector of the economy. Prior to the crash, Qatar, like the rest of the Gulf, was looking to real estate, education, and to a lesser extent tourism, to diversify its economy. However, in 2008 the real estate sector crashed, and mega-projects in Qatar and the rest of the Gulf were mothballed. Glossy skyscrapers stand empty in the financial center, and uninhabited estates in the embassy district look like stony monochrome palaces on a lifeless, colorless moon.

You can imagine that for someone tasked with opening restaurants in Doha and throughout the Middle East, this was troubling. But in 2008, it was still just a business challenge—albeit a more difficult one than I had expected. I sent for my family to join me in Doha. This was going to be a long-term, if not permanent, move for us.

To this day, Doha's skyline is littered with unfinished buildings and vacant skyscrapers. Even the emir was building a 90-story tower in the West Bay. The rent revenue from this building was to be part of his zakat (a religious duty for Muslims to give to charity) and it was dedicated to the city of Jerusalem. But the project was mothballed, along with countless others scattered throughout the city.

Throughout the crisis, Qatari authorities sought to protect the local banking sector. The government injected billions of the dollars into domestic banks, first by purchasing all of the banks' stock portfolios at book value, and then by direct investment by the Qatar Investment Authority in the banks to increase their liquidity.

The government would also, from time to time, forgive certain bank obligations for Qataris. The banks would log the government funding as income in their books and continue to show a profit. In addition, banks rarely called a bad loan in Qatar; they would find creative ways to make the loan appear solvent in their books. It was all a charade, supported by the government and the central bank, to make the banking sector look unaffected by the financial crisis while banks throughout the rest of the world spiraled out of control.

Qatar's GDP rebounded in 2010, largely due to the increase in oil prices. Qatar's economic policy is focused on developing the country's non-associated natural gas reserves and increasing private and foreign investment in non-energy sectors, but oil and gas still account for more than 50% of the GDP, roughly 85% of export earnings, and 70% of government revenues.

Oil and gas alone have made Qatar the highest per-capita income country—ahead of Liechtenstein—and have also made it the country with the lowest unemployment rate. Proven oil reserves of 25 billion barrels should enable continued output at current levels for 57 years. Qatar's proven reserves of natural gas exceed 25 trillion cubic meters, about 14% of the world total and third largest in the world.

Qatar's successful 2022 World Cup bid will likely accelerate large-scale infrastructure projects, such as Qatar's metro system and the Qatar–Bahrain causeway (which will be one of the longest bridges ever built, if it does get built), and these projects will all be funded by oil and gas revenues.

Still early on in my time in Qatar, billions of dollars were being invested in the energy sector, and the Al Jazeera news network had put Qatar on the world's stage. Doha, the capital of the tiny emirate, was in a construction boom that rivaled regional powerhouses Dubai and Abu Dhabi.

In fact, at that time, the region as a whole was burgeoning after years of suffering from depressed oil prices. The Arab Gulf countries, consisting of Saudi Arabia, Kuwait, The United Arab Emirates, Qatar, Bahrain and Oman, were experiencing an unprecedented burst of energy. Oil prices had reached over $100 a barrel, dramatically up from a low of $18 in 1998. Governments couldn't spend the revenue fast enough and embarked on ambitious projects in every sector from energy to infrastructure, education, housing, healthcare and transportation. Capital from all over the world was flowing into the region. There was a fierce competition between these countries and their rulers to outdo each other, to build the biggest, the tallest and the largest, even if some of their "accomplishments" made no economic sense and were not sustainable. The banks couldn't give away money fast enough, and there was no such thing as a harebrained idea. For proof, just look at the ski slope in the desert, man-made islands shaped like palm trees and the world map, the world's tallest building, the world's largest mall and the proposed underwater hotel. Five star hotels no longer offered sufficient luxury, so seven star hotels were introduced to fill the needs of the region's nouveaux riches.

Twenty- and thirty-something Gulf locals were assigned titles and put into executive positions, regardless of whether they were suited for the positions or not. They surrounded themselves with high-priced Brits, Americans and Europeans who fanned their egos and facilitated their whims.

When I first arrived in Doha, the city had just hosted the Asia Games the previous year, in 2006. Not only had the games been lackluster, but the anticipated infrastructure expansion to accommodate the multitude of visiting fans never materialized, and neither did the fans themselves.

It didn't matter. Qatar's PR machine, led by Emir Hamad bin Khalifa al-Thani and his foreign minister, Sheikh Hamad bin Jabor al-Thani, was active and continued to use the country's newfound wealth to promote Qatar as a modern, tolerant country and a welcoming society. It was anything but.

The Emir continued on his ambitious agenda to transform Qatar into a regional and international player. With an endless supply of gas dollars, it was easy to find eager beneficiaries to help him achieve his goals. Qatar continued hosting conferences and international meetings and kept up the charade for the rest of the world to see.

Qatar's Emir is benevolent, as despots go, but it remains one of the most totalitarian regimes in the world. Security services allow no dissent and keep a watchful eye on everything that goes on in the emirate. Political freedom is not tolerated in any shape or form, yet the government regularly underwrites the cost of conferences on "Democracy," flies people in on the revamped Qatar Airways, and puts participants up at the new Ritz-Carlton Doha—all at the government's expense.

The Qatari government kept up the vision that Qatar was open for business. It strived to be the new frontier for expatriates looking for high-paying jobs. This was the Qatar I had bought into and thought I had moved to. Into this dangerous mirage I blindly walked, even bringing my family with me.

CHAPTER 6: THE OPPORTUNITY OF A LIFETIME

Years back, I had my first experience with Qatar when, by chance, I met Ambassador Badr al-Dafa, Qatar's Ambassador to Washington. It was 2001 and I was working as the Executive Director of the American Arab Chamber of Commerce, a Dearborn, Michigan-based business organization whose mission was to promote Arab-American business owners in particular and the Arab-American community in general. It was shortly after the 9/11 tragedy, and we were looking for ways to work with the Arab world and Arab governments to build a better relationship between the Arab world and the United States, using the Arab-American community as a bridge.

I had actually met Ambassador al-Dafa once before, in the early 70s. He was a student at Western Michigan University in Kalamazoo, where I would visit my aunts during breaks from school. My Aunt Naziha owned the Variety Delicatessen. She used to serve Arab food to the small community of Arab students, so it became the hangout for many homesick students. Aunt Wanda and her husband owned M & W tailor shop next door. I would spend my vacations working between the two shops.

Thirty years later, Ambassador al-Dafa was very worldly and enlightened, and he saw the importance of the Arab-American community as a potential bridge between the U.S. and Arab worlds. He invested his time, effort and financial resources provided by his government to support our efforts.

After the events of 9/11, Qatar was one of the few Arab governments that took an active interest in the Arab-American community and provided financial support for our initiatives and projects. I first visited Qatar in 2002 as a guest of the Foreign Minister Hamad bin Jassim al-Thani, to attend one of the first Democracy conferences held in conjunction with the Brookings Institution. At first sight, Doha, with its sweeping bay and its palm-tree-lined cornice, was very appealing. You could sense that the country lacked the development taking place in Dubai or Abu Dhabi, but still, you could see the potential that Doha had to offer.

That same year, Amre Moussa, the Secretary General of the League of Arab States, introduced me to Abdullah Bin Hamid al-Attiyah, Qatar's Oil Minister, at a World Economic Forum meeting in Geneva. The meeting was held to introduce the WEF's economic and human development report on the Arab world.

Minister al-Attiyah was warm and friendly. He came off like a favorite uncle. He had attended school at Port Huron Community College in Port Huron, Michigan and had an affinity for everything from Michigan. He was also an expert on Lebanon, loved everything Lebanese and was called the "Lebanese Minister" in the Qatari Government. Since I was a Lebanese American from Michigan, we hit it off immediately. From that meeting, we formed a friendship and I continued to visit him every time I visited Doha with a delegation.

The American Arab Chamber was also working with the Arab Community Center for Economic and Social Services (ACCESS) to raise money for a National Arab American Museum that ACCESS was spearheading. After 9/11, Arab-American community leaders in Michigan decided that we needed a venue that told our story in the United States. We wanted Americans to gain a better understanding of the contributions of Arab-Americans to America. There were fifteen thousand museums in the U.S., but not one that told our immigrant story or the contribution of Arabs to civilization.

We had budgeted fifteen million dollars for the project, the most ever raised by the Arab-American community for a project, and we set out to raise that sum. Ahmad Chebbani, chairman of the Arab American Chamber; Ish Ahmed, executive director of ACCESS; and Hassan Jaber, deputy director of ACCESS, and I traveled the Arab world, raising some of the money for the project. The majority of the funding came from the Arab-American community and American foundations in the form of grants.

Amre Moussa was one of the drivers of our efforts in the Arab world, and he used his position as secretary general of the League of Arab States to open doors for us. He pushed Arab leaders to contribute. Minister al-Attiyah and Ambassador al-Dafa helped secure a gift of $1 million from the government of Qatar for the project. This generous donation contributed to my positive thoughts about Qatar, of course.

In 2002 Secretary General Moussa, Ahmad and I conceived a plan to hold an economic forum to help build better understanding between the United States and Arab world, using the strong economic ties that existed as the basis. So we spent a year and a half traveling the Arab world, building support and raising funds for this event. Once again, Qatar, through the efforts of Ambassador al-Dafa, contributed $500,000 to our effort.

Thus in September of 2003, the first U.S.-Arab Economic Forum was held in Detroit. The three-day event was a tremendous success. With over fifteen hundred participants, the forum brought together Secretary of State Colin Powell and Secretary of Energy Spencer Abraham (an Arab-American and former U.S. senator from Michigan); foreign ministers from Saudi Arabia, Egypt, Bahrain and Qatar; the oil ministers from Saudi Arabia and Qatar; the chairmen or CEOs of ExxonMobil, Chevron, ConocoPhillips and Marathon; and the chairmen of GM, Ford, HP and Intel. At the gala banquet, the dais was impressive. Six of the "Fortune Ten" CEOs were in attendance, hobnobbing with the ministers. Never had the Arab-American community held such a monumental event. This event raised the profile of our community and my position as a leader in the community.

I continued to lead delegations to the region, with Qatar as one of the main destinations. Through my contacts, Qatar would help underwrite the trips or provide accommodation or logistical support for the delegation. I continued to build my contacts in the country and watch it grow and develop with every visit.

Every time we visited, we experienced something new, like one of the Qatar Foundation's endeavors, the multi-billion dollar Education City, a mission spearheaded by the emir's second wife Sheikha Mozah al-Misned. With substantial financial incentives, Qatar lured major American educational institutions like Cornell, Texas A & M, and Carnegie-Mellon to open branch campuses in Qatar. Their presence in Qatar will be explored in greater depth in the appendix.

Qatar was on the move and it seemed the place to be.

In 2004, two former Arab American Chamber board members, Assam (Sam) Sheikh and Abdulla al-Jufairi, moved to Qatar. Sam was a successful local businessman who owned a local company, PCSI, and had made a small fortune supplying project management services to General Motors. Abdulla was a Qatari who went to study in Michigan, married a

Lebanese girl and stayed in Michigan. He was one of the few people to emigrate from Qatar. Coincidently, his wife's father used to be the cook at my Aunt Naziha's restaurant in Kalamazoo.

In 2005, I was recruited by Sam to run PCSI in Michigan. I resigned as the executive director of the Chamber and took on the position of CEO at PCSI. That same year, I was elected to the board of the Chamber as the vice chairman. I continued to be active in the Arab-American community, taking delegations of elected officials and businessman to the region.

Michigan's economy was entering into a recession, and PCSI operations suffered with the slowdown in the auto industry. Sam and Abdulla had set up PCSI Global in Qatar, and that company was booming. I continued to monitor Qatar's explosive growth during every visit.

The Chamber decided to hold a second U.S.-Arab Economic Forum in Houston in 2006. Houston also has a substantial Arab-American population, and the city's connection to the oil industry made it an obvious choice to host the forum. Once again, I traveled to the Arab countries trying to build support for the forum. Once again, Minister al-Attiyah played a pivotal role. The forum also received the support of Nijad Fares of Houston, one of the most important leaders in the Arab-American community. The Chamber had honored Nijad several years earlier as its national businessman of the year. He was the son of Issam Fares, one of Lebanon's greatest leaders and a self-made billionaire. Nijad's support, as one of Houston's most respected businessmen, ensured that the forum would receive the necessary backing from Houston's political and corporate leaders.

I also had the privilege to meet H.H. Turki al-Faisal, the newly appointed ambassador of Saudi Arabia. Prince Turki is one of the most charming and intelligent men I have ever met. In his short tenure as the Kingdom's Ambassador, he actively engaged the Arab-American community, something his predecessor Prince Bandar bin Sultan never did.

Bandar's nickname was Bandar Bush; he focused all his energies in Washington, and in particular, with the White House. He had no time for the Arab-American community, and America to him consisted of the Beltway. Prince Turki was the antithesis of this. He traveled the country, meeting middle class America and the Arab-American community. He also saw the importance of the forum and threw his support behind our efforts.

During this period, Ambassador al-Dafa was recalled to Doha, and a new ambassador, Nasser al-Khalifa, was appointed. Ambassador al-Khalifa, also a product of Western Michigan University, was appointed the Qatari representative to Washington. He was the opposite of al-Dafa. He gave the impression that he didn't want to be in the U.S. and preferred his previous posting in London. He also seemed to have something of a dual personality; one day he was your best friend, and the next day he didn't know you. I would later find this trait in several of the other Qataris I dealt with.

In June 2006, Israel devastated Lebanon with a war against Hezbollah, virtually wiping out Lebanon's infrastructure and decimating my ancestral village of Bint Jbail. Shortly after the war stopped, through the Arab American Chamber, I took a delegation of Arab-American leaders, press and Congressional staffers to see firsthand the ramifications of the war. During that visit, Qatar's Emir announced that he was going to rebuild several of the villages destroyed by the war, and Bint Jbail was one of them. Needless to say, this gave me an even more positive attitude towards Qatar.

At the end of that year, I went on a visit to Qatar at the request of Sam Sheikh; he wanted me to see again how the country was booming. In February of 2007, Donald Jordon, a Detroit native, had moved to Qatar with Abdullah al-Jufairi to start an investment company called Atlantic Capital. In June of 2006, Atlantic had raised 100 million riyals ($26,000,000) and created a restaurant holding company called Wataniya. The company's eighty-six shareholders were some of the biggest names in Qatar.

Donald asked if I would be interested in moving to Qatar and running the company. I discussed it with Maysa and we decided that I would go to Qatar and try it out. If things worked out, the family would follow. So in April of 2007, I made the fateful decision to go and work in Qatar, and over a year later, in July of 2008, my family joined me.

I arrived in Doha in the middle of the night on April 6, 2007. The driver for Atlantic Capital was there to pick me up. He drove me to what would be my apartment for the next four months. It was a two-bedroom flat located in the al-Sadd district of Doha. The apartment was spacious, but due to the heat, it let in very little sunlight. I hardly slept that night in anticipation of new life and role.

The next morning, Donald Jordan picked me up and we set off to Wataniya's corporate offices in the Bin Omran section of Doha, near the studios of Al Jazeera, about two miles down the road from my apartment. Wataniya occupied the second floor of a small three-story office building, with Abdullah al-Jufairi's office occupying about a third of the space. The first floor was occupied by PCSI Global and Sam Sheikh's office. Era Realty, PCSI's IT department and Protocol, all companies associated with Abdullah, occupied the mezzanine. The third floor was occupied by PCSI's finance department and the building's landlord, Nasser al-Kabi. Nasser al-Kabi was in the military during the day and a businessman in the evenings. This was a common trend among the small Qatari population. Many worked in government posts but also owned businesses. This was easy for them to do because the demand for Qatari partners is so high—as I mentioned, foreign business owners are required to have a 51% Qatari partner.

Donald called a meeting and introduced me to the staff that Atlantic had hired. From its inception, the company was managed by Atlantic. Abdullah was Atlantic's Chairman. He was also the vice chairman and managing director of Wataniya and was the person I would report to. The main person in charge of Wataniya's day-to-day operations was the COO, an Irishman named Andrew Sharp. He was the first person hired by Atlantic. He had previously worked for Compass, one of the world's largest food service companies. Andrew and Atlantic, mainly Donald, had hired the balance of the twelve person staff I met that morning.

Andrew and Donald had bought franchise rights for Sbarro in Qatar, the UAE, Bahrain, Kuwait and Oman for $820,000, despite the fact that Sbarro was a dying brand in the United States. It had been tried before in Qatar and failed. They also obtained the rights for Mongolian Barbeque in London for the Middle East for $225,000 and eventually went on to buy the rights for Abdel Wahab (a Lebanese Restaurant) and Duo (a French and Italian restaurant) from Ghia in Lebanon, Buddha Bar for Qatar, and Rainforest Café in Cairo. They signed an MOU with Outback Steakhouse for Qatar and paid a $100,000 deposit. They also purchased the rights for the Landry brands, which is the parent company for Rainforest Café for Qatar. They had spent $1,700,000 on franchise rights.

In addition, they formed a Joint Venture with Qatar National Hotels (QNH) to establish a catering company in Qatar. QNH is a government-owned company that owned and operated the majority of the hotels in Qatar, including the Marriott, Ritz, Sheraton and others. Wataniya invested a little over $2 million in the venture. Atlantic took over $1,400,000 in fees from Wataniya for the eleven months it ran the operation. By the time I arrived, Atlantic had spent $6,800,000 of the initial $27 million paid in capital and had not opened a single outlet. So I began my tenure as CEO with a bloated staff, no operational restaurants, third-rate franchises and twenty five percent of the company's capital already spent.

I dove in and began to gain a better understanding of the company and the country. I did a quick assessment of the operations and the staff and quickly saw that the company was not established on a solid foundation. The staff was not of the caliber needed to build a world-class food and beverage operation. In fact, by the time I left, all but one of the original staff was gone. I had terminated them all.

A few days into the job, I had my first experience with the Qatari sponsorship system. The company's HR manager had informed me that I needed to get my residency permit. I also found out from her that Wataniya did not have a work visa for a U.S. citizen, but they had applied for one. After pressing her further, she told me that companies are awarded a certain number of work visas that vary by the type of nationalities they can hire. These restrictions come from the Labor Department and are based on the nature of the company and the type of workers that are needed. For instance, you might ask for a hundred visas for workers from India, and the labor department might come back and give you thirty visas for workers from Nepal.

As I delved deeper into this visa process, I found out that when you hire a new employee, you have to recruit from abroad; it is very difficult to hire from the local markets. Further, all foreign workers in Qatar are legally required to be the under the sponsorship of a Qatari. Even international companies require a local sponsor. For instance, all the American universities operating in Qatar, e.g., Texas A&M, Cornell, and Georgetown, are all under the sponsorship of the Qatar Foundation. If a professor or employee wants to leave the country for a visit, he or she needs an exit permit from the Qatar Foundation.

In essence, the local sponsor owns you. He can, at anytime, cancel your visa for no cause, have you deported and bar you from working in Qatar for two years—even if you complete your contract and wish to transfer to a new employer in Qatar. You must first obtain a release from your previous sponsor. If he refuses, you are forced to leave the country and not work in Qatar for a period of two years.

Doha is littered with stories of people who have worked for a Qatari company for years, and when they try to move to a better position, they are denied that basic right by their Qatari sponsor. Once you have a residence permit stamped on your passport, your sponsor makes all your decisions for you. You will need his permission to open a bank account, rent a house or apartment, obtain a driver's license or even buy a car. And what is even more degrading and humiliating, if you wish to bring your family to live with you, while you work and contribute to building the country's economy, you must first be a certain classification of employee, then you need your sponsor's permission. But what is most repressive is that your sponsor must provide you an exit permit if you want to travel outside of Qatar. Most Qatari sponsors provide a single exit permit, instead of multi exit permits, thus forcing you to seek his permission every time you wish to leave.

During my time in Qatar, I heard countless unfortunate stories of people who had family emergencies but were not able to leave because their sponsor was not in Qatar to grant them an exit permit. Other stories included expatriates who went to the airport to travel, only to be turned back because there was a problem with their exit permit.

Qatar and Saudi Arabia have the most repressive sponsorship systems in the Gulf; however, the entire Gulf region treats expatriates as commodities.

After Wataniya was able to convert one of their visas to the category of a U.S. Manager visa, the HR manager came to me with an employment contract. She told me I needed to sign it so they could begin the paperwork for my residency permit. The contract she presented did not include all the terms that I had agreed to with Atlantic, the company that I considered had actually hired me. After I raised this concern with her and Abdullah, they said this was just a standard contract that needed to be filed with the Labor Department. So I signed the labor contract and began the residency permit process.

Like all companies in Qatar, Wataniya had a person serving as *mandoob*—a person whose sole job is to move the company's paperwork through the various Qatari agencies and government ministries. You cannot operate in Qatar without a mandoob. Generally these roles are filled by lower-caste Qataris, Egyptians, Sudanese or Somalis.

Wataniya's mandoob took me for my physical examination. If you have ever seen cattle being herded, this is what it's like in the Qatari medical exam facility.

After I passed all the tests and received my residence permit, I was able to get a Qatari driver's license, and the mandoob also secured a letter of permission from Wataniya to open a bank account. Knowing that the legal formalities were completed, it was time to get to work.

About a month into the job, Donald took me to meet Dr. Khalid bin Mohamed al-Attiyah, Wataniya's chairman. Khalid was a prominent Qatari lawyer whose father was the founder of the Qatari Armed forces, and he himself had served as a pilot in the Qatari Air Force. He owned a law firm and was also at that time the chairman of the National Committee for Human Rights, the organization that was established to protect the

right of foreign workers in Qatar and ensure that Qatar was in compli-
ance with international human rights.

The meeting with Khalid lasted about fifteen minutes. He said he was
impressed with my resume and wondered whether I thought I could
handle the position. I told him I would do my best and would like his
support and guidance, as well as the support and guidance of the board.
However, he never took an active role in the company from the beginning
to the end of my tenure. In fact, the board had only met once in October
2006, prior to my arrival. The next board meeting did not take place until
February 2008, almost a year after I started. All in all, the board met four
times during my tenure at Wataniya, leaving my interaction with the
board limited to Abdullah, who was assigned as the board's representative. The corporate charter and Qatari law clearly stipulate that the
board is obliged to meet six times per year.

As I dove into my job, it seemed odd to me that that the company had
so much staff yet did not have any restaurants open. The only thing the
staff was doing was managing a Lebanese restaurant called Awtar for
Abdullah. It seemed that Abdullah and Sam had built this restaurant for
themselves while Abdullah was running Wataniya.

I approached Abdullah and Sam and explained that this was a major
conflict of interest and said that they should sell the restaurant at cost to
Wataniya. So in July 2007, Abdullah sold the restaurant to Wataniya for
$630,000; this became Wataniya's first outlet. Ironically, even with all
the staff available, the restaurant was still not managed properly.

I started talking with the staff to see what their roles were and what
they were working on. I dealt mainly with Andrew, the COO. He filled
me in on the projects and also let me know that they had just signed a
deal to rent a store on Nasir Street, a building owned by Sheikh Hamad
bin Jassim al-Thani (who serves as both prime minister and foreign minister). It was located on a good commercial avenue and would appear to
be a desirable location for one of the brands.

Wataniya's operations manager had found this location, and according to Andrew, Wataniya was paying $186,000 for the location from the
tenant (key money). I inquired if the location was approved for use as a
food facility and whether the building was scheduled to be demolished,
as many of Doha's older commercial districts were being torn down to
make room for new buildings and centers. According to the operations
manager, they had received confirmation from the prime minister's office
that it was OK, and that he had no objections to the transfer of the lease.
So based on this information, they proceeded with the acquisition.

Several months later, when we submitted our plans for the outlet and requested a letter of no objection from the landlord to obtain the permit, we were informed that the building was going to be demolished. When I told the chairman and Abdullah about this and recommended legal action, they refused, insisting they were not about to sue the prime minister. They said the monies invested were a loss.

Donald Jordan also briefed me on the project in Egypt. It seems that Wataniya had bought the rights for Rainforest Café in Cairo from al-Swadi Group. They had also retained the general manager hired by al-Swadi, who was a former Four Seasons food and beverage manager. Atlantic had put their construction manager in charge of overseeing the construction of the project, which came with a seventeen-thousand square-foot location in City Star mall in Cairo, the largest mall in Africa and one of the busiest in Egypt. Atlantic hired an architecture firm from Minnesota to design the restaurant. The same firm had also designed a majority of the Rainforest Cafés for Landry.

The team had been holding meetings for several months prior to my arrival, yet I learned that the legal framework for the project was not complete and little progress had been made. So in May of 2007, I brought in a new project manager for the Rainforest Café in Egypt, Ameen Kassam.

Ameen and I had worked together at PCSI in the U.S. He had grown up in Windsor, Canada, with my wife Maysa. He had moved to Qatar about a year earlier and was working with Sam at PCSI Global. I asked that Ameen be loaned to Wataniya because he was honest and good at what he did. Shortly after that, he moved to Egypt and began to lay the foundation, working with the general manager and his staff to get the restaurant built.

When Ameen arrived in Egypt, he discovered several problems. Donald Jordon had hired an American law firm, who in turn had delegated the project to their local affiliate. They had not set up the company as a tourist operation, which would have exempted it from import duties. Neither had they set it up as a foreign investment vehicle. Atlantic's failure in establishing the operations in Egypt would go on to cost Wataniya over $1 million. In addition, by hiring a local firm through an American firm, we were paying U.S. attorney rates for Egyptian lawyers.

After a while, we fixed what we could and got the operation going. Once the operation in Egypt was on track and progress was being made, I focused on Qatar.

In my early days in Doha I reached out to a friend, Sheikh Jaber bin Youseff al-Thani, someone I had met on my visits to Qatar. He was the

Chief of Staff for his uncle Sheikh Hamad bin Jassim al-Thani ("HJB"), the prime minister and foreign minister. Sheikh Jaber introduced me to his business manager, who took a keen interest in me and Wataniya. His business manager was a typical Lebanese hustler. He had previously worked for the Lebanese Christian militia leader who was implicated in the Sabra and Shatila massacres of Lebanese and Palestinian civilians during the Lebanese Civil War.

In fact, this business manager is prominently mentioned in the book *Cobra* by Robert Hatem, which is about the Lebanese Civil War. It seems that he ran afoul of the Syrians, who arrested him and tortured him, leaving him with a severe stutter to this day.

Through Sheikh Jaber and his dubious business manager, I met a very successful Qatari businessman who had made a fortune developing real estate for Qatari sheikhs. One of his projects was an apartment building in the West Bay section of Doha that was built to house visitors for the 2006 Asian Games. This was one of the few projects that was actually completed in time for the games, and the developer made a fortune due to that fact.

I negotiated a deal to rent two restaurant spaces in the building. I also rented an apartment for myself for a monthly rate that was considered a good deal for Doha.

I submitted the proposal to Abdullah for a second-floor poolside restaurant and a restaurant on the twenty-ninth floor. It would be a ten-thousand square-foot fine dining establishment with two large balconies with stunning views of Doha, in the heart of Doha's new high-rise business district. It was a prime location targeting the executives who worked and lived in the area.

I then went on to rent several more locations and began to fulfill the company's mission of becoming a food and beverage powerhouse in the region, as instructed by the board.

Atlantic had no strategic plan or development plan for the company. They just raised the money—and I think they themselves hadn't expected how easy it would be to raise the capital. But having raised the money, they didn't have a day-after strategy.

During my tenure at Wataniya, I opened over thirty outlets in Qatar, Dubai and Egypt. I created joint ventures in Dubai and Lebanon and purchased Wataniya's most valuable franchise rights: Kabab-Ji, al-Rifai, Chopsticks, Caribou Coffee, Rainforest Café Dubai, Abdul Rahman al-Hallab. I also created four company concepts, NY Deli, American Grill, Pita Fresh and Restaurant 29. This was done with the full knowledge of the board and based on the premise that the company needed to begin to pay a dividend to the shareholders, who were getting anxious. They had invested substantial amounts of money into the operation and were demanding a return on their investment. I was eager to get them that return, and so we embarked on an aggressive expansion.

CHAPTER 7: ARABIAN NIGHTMARES

Hamad bin Abdullah al-Attiyah is the cousin of the chairman, Minister Khalid bin Mohamed al-Attiyah. In July he had been appointed by the board of Wataniya as an advisor to the chairman, with the intention that he would be the next chairman. He was tasked with overseeing the company and reporting his findings to the board. His mission, on behalf of the board, was to assess the financial situation of the company and use his influence to raise additional capital.

I had known Hamad for many years, having met him in Detroit in 2005. He was also a cousin and the brother-in-law of Abdullah bin Hamad al-Attiyah, the Qatari Deputy Prime Minister and Oil Minister. Because of my relationship with Minister al-Attiyah and because the Emir of Qatar's mother was an al-Attiyah, I had the impression that the al-Attiyahs were honorable in their dealings—people who could be trusted. This was certainly not the case with these two. Hamad proved to be malicious and evil, and I believe that my captivity was the direct result of this man's actions.

Hamad and I clashed several times following his appointment. From the moment I began my tenure at Wataniya, he had taken a keen interest in the company. He would call me at all hours if he went to one of the restaurants and thought it was overstaffed or if the meal didn't suit him. He was the type of person who was quick to complain or criticize but never gave a compliment or kind word.

He was also the first to let me know that the shareholders were getting anxious—that we needed to grow quickly and the company needed to start paying dividends. He would pick me up and drive me around Doha, telling me we needed to open outlets in various parts of the city. He had knowledge of everything we did, every brand we acquired, as well as the costs associated with the restaurant build-outs. On several occasions, he met us in Cairo and saw the progress at the Rainforest Café we were building there. He never expressed any concerns or voiced any objections.

As I began to interact with Hamad more, I realized this man's portrayal of himself as a distinguished member of Qatari society was a farce. He had background as an officer in the Qatari Army, but he was also a trained engineer; yet many people I met knew him and nobody had anything good to say about him. When the board appointed him to this position, one board member actually resigned.

When Hamad retired from the army, he was sent to Q-Tel (Qatar's telephone and mobile provider), where he was removed because no one could tolerate him. After Q-Tel and until his forced retirement, he was appointed as the general manager of the Qatar Pension and Retirement Authority.

His respectable façade didn't match his shady dealings. Hamad, I would later find out, was a silent partner with Abdullah al-Jufairi, Wataniya's Vice Chairman and Managing Director, in Atlantic Capital. His shares, as I heard, were held by his nephew, who would later be appointed Minister of State of the Interior.

Atlantic was managed by Donald Jordon, and it had formed Wataniya and raised the initial capital. Hamad was also al-Jufairi's partner in a company called Tasheed Real Estate and ERA Real Estate Qatar. This is where matters get murky: Why was Hamad removed from the pension fund? It seems while general manager of the pension fund, he was using Atlantic to manage a part of the fund's money. In addition, he had a company in Kuwait, Global Finance House, which was managing a substantial amount of the pension fund's money. In turn, Global invested in Wataniya and bought Hamad's shares in Tasheed at an inflated price.

When Hamad called me into his office one morning in early October 2009, I sensed that something was wrong. He had brought in an Egyptian-American management consultant to assist him in assessing the company. Simultaneously, the chairman, Khalid al-Attiyah, had hired an internal auditor to review the company's books. Neither of these consultants was talking to me, and I let them work uninterrupted, confident that the company's books were clean and I had nothing to fear.

During the fateful meeting with Hamad, he leveled several accusations at me, including mismanaging the company. He said I would be responsible for the fifty million riyals (13.7 million dollars) in losses and I would be blamed because the many other people associated with the company were too important. He also said I might even go to jail, because someone had to take the fall.

Shocked, I told him I wouldn't be his or anyone's scapegoat and that there was nothing wrong with the company. I also reminded him that I hadn't received a salary since May. I had voluntarily stopped taking one because the company had been going through some cash flow shortfalls, and since I was in charge of paying the employees, I had decided to pay the employees before paying myself. I had put all my efforts into this company to open over thirty outlets in a little over two years.

I told him the company needed a financial injection to complete the projects, and that we had begun to reduce the operating costs. As is standard, restaurants that were newly opened needed time to generate the cash flow necessary to sustain the operations. I could see the venom in his eyes. I knew, at that point, I was in trouble and that things were going to get ugly.

Already that evening my finance manager, Elaine Dib, called me and told me she had heard that the chairman, Khalid al-Attiyah, had asked the HR manager to cancel my exit permit.

I had heard many stories of people being held in Qatar and not being able to leave, so I immediately packed a small suitcase and headed to the airport. I bought a ticket to Beirut, intending to leave the country before it was too late.

When I reached the customs counter, I was informed that my exit permit was not valid and I needed to get one. I was stuck.

The next day I went to Hamad's office and submitted my resignation, in a letter addressed to Chairman Khalid, not alerting him to the fact that I was aware that they had canceled my exit permit.

My last day of employment with Wataniya will be Saturday, October 30, 2009. I regret that my tenure has to end without being able to see Wataniya flourish. I have worked hard over the last two-and-a-half years to try and build a world-class food services operation. However, I am confident in the foundation that was laid, and once the funding shortfall is overcome and the restaurants are open, Wataniya will achieve the results you desire.

My decisions to leave are based on many factors, most notably that I value my integrity and my accomplishments. In addition, the following factors have played a major role:

I have not received a salary in over four months.

I have not had any of my expenses paid.

I have not had my children's school tuition paid for this school year.

My accommodation rent has not been paid in over four months.

I have on several occasions been subjected to comments that I have acted in an inappropriate financial manner or stolen from this company.

I have been informed that several high ranking government officials wish to put me in jail.

I have been kept in the dark as to the future and potential funding sources.

As I stated in my last month, I know that you have lost faith in me. That is your right, for the company today is not where you or I want it be or where it should be. I have made some decisions that in hindsight, I would have done differently. However, accusations and implications that I have stolen from this company, I will not tolerate. As you have stated on several occasions that you have your reputation and dignity, I too have my reputation and honor and will not allow anyone to sully it in any way, regardless of who he or she might be.

Hamad read the letter and said he would not accept it. He also said he would deny any of the information attributed to him.

He told me I had to stay on until the company's general assembly meeting, which was going to be held in November (about two months later), open Rainforest Café Dubai, and then I could leave. He also told me that if I refused, by Qatari law he could have me arrested as having absconded from work.

At that moment I felt the world cave in on me. I realized that the al-Attiyahs had no intention of properly capitalizing the company. They were looking for someone to point the finger at for the financial mess. Their prime concern was to protect the reputation of Minister Khalid bin Mohamed al-Attiyah, then chairman of Wataniya. They did not want the shareholders to blame him or tarnish his image.

I went back to my office, so mad I was shaking. I started to think about what I could do. From that point on, I was isolated from the company affairs.

I would come to work and sit in the office. The consultant Hamad had hired was running the company, and I had minimal interaction with the staff and Hamad. I was no longer involved in company discussions. I was only approached by the consultant when he needed information. The situation was so bad, and I was under so much stress, that I came down with shingles, a painful skin condition caused by stress. It took me over three months to recover.

Most of the staff who reported to me quickly switched their allegiance to the new management team. Only six staff members remained loyal to me; they became my eyes and ears in the company. They would let me know what was happening, what was being said, and what Hamad and Khalid were thinking. Through them, I was beginning to understand how things would unfold—they were going to try to shift the blame for anything that had gone wrong with the company onto me.

What was most shocking was how fast some of the people who worked for me turned against me. They began to question the decisions I had made and tried to build favor with Hamad his consultant. For most of the staff, this was understandable; they just saw the writing on the wall and had no other option but to please the new management because their livelihood depended on it. I have no problems with those who neither hurt me nor helped me. However, the most shocking were those who had, prior to all this, been feeding misinformation to Khalid and Hamad behind my back.

One of them was a secretary when I started. I had taken her under my wing and guided her career at the company, promoting her as positions became available. However, I later found out that she had been relaying misinformation to Khalid al-Attiyah about me. She had convinced him that I was embezzling from the company, though she had no proof. She was just an opportunist trying to curry favor with the chairman.

Another was someone I had known for over nine years. I found out he had been spreading rumors about me to everyone he met, from the first day I brought him in to work for me. Because of his position, he had run across Hamad and began to feed him lies. He convinced Hamad, who in turn convinced Khalid, that I had embezzled money from the company and bought the Fairlane Club in Dearborn, Michigan, as well as a house and several businesses from the money I took from Wataniya. I believe he is the one who came up with the fifty-million riyal figure that I "took."

In addition to the damage he was doing to me in Qatar, I also figured out that he was feeding rumors back home in Michigan that I was in jail, or that I was under investigation in Qatar, or that I had a travel ban. Friends would call, concerned, because they had heard rumors that I was in trouble, and unbeknownst to me, it was all coming from a man I had gone out of my way to help.

With the damage to my reputation done and the al-Attiyahs determined to focus all the blame on me, I needed to find a way to protect myself. With the help of those who remained loyal to me, I began to assemble any and all documents that might be useful, in the event they chose to pursue legal action. Mind you, at that point I had not received my salary for five months.

Elaine was the most helpful, though she had nothing to gain by helping. In fact, quite the contrary: she had everything to lose. She had started at Wataniya about the same time I had, as an assistant accountant. The finance manager, at that time, had been hired by Atlantic and had no qualifications to be the finance manager for any company. He would pay anything anyone told him to pay. He kept the company books on an excel spreadsheet and the company's financial records in a cardboard box. Every time I tried to get him to explain anything, he would begin to stutter. I realized quickly that he had to go and began to search for a replacement. Wataniya, at that time, had no restaurants operational and the finances were handled primarily by Atlantic. So at least his damage was minimal and could be contained.

When I first met Elaine, she had just moved to Qatar with her new husband. She was not more than 23 or 24 years old. I really didn't think she would amount to much, but she proved me wrong; immediately after she started at Wataniya, she came to my office to complain about how the finance manager was handling the books. She had identified the very issues that I had concerns about.

I asked HR to give me her resume and studied it further. I called Elaine and asked her what she would do if she was in charge of financing. She gave me her vision of how she would set up the accounting office. I was impressed by how on the ball she was. She had a sharp-as-a-tack financial mind. So I made the decision then that she would be the finance manager.

I asked her to begin to take over the responsibility and put together the team she wanted. She set out to establish the financial department, hiring and training her first employee. She set up the policies and procedures, implemented the new software and organized the company records.

She was my secret weapon. People would underestimate her and let their guard down, but little did they know, they were dealing with a pit bull. By the time I left, she was the second-highest-paid employee in the company, yet she put it all on the line to help me. I had nothing to offer and the Attiyahs had promised her to keep her on, due to the fact that she was not "tainted" by me. Yet she chose to do the right thing and help me. If it weren't for her, I wouldn't have had some of the documents that protected me against the unsubstantiated allegations. I will be forever in her debt and words cannot express my gratitude.

In late October, Khalid called for a general assembly meeting for November 22, 2009.

Based on the construction schedule, the Dubai Rainforest Café would be open on November 23, so according to our previous discussion, my last day at the company would be the 23rd. Based on this information, I sent Hamad a letter on October 29, notifying him of my last day and asking that the finance department prepare my end-of-service calculations. In the meantime, I was secretly assembling as many documents as possible without raising suspicion.

The general assembly meeting went forward on November 22, 2009, and the board held a meeting prior to it, which I was excluded from participating in, although I was present. The board did not even give me the courtesy of allowing me to address any concerns that they might have had about my tenure or actions, even though I had informed Mr. Hamad al-Attiyah verbally and in writing that I would be happy to answer any questions that the board might have. For the rest of my time in Qatar, such a meeting never materialized.

After my last day of employment, I requested that the company provide me with my end-of-service statement and release of employment, as I had fulfilled his employment contract. From my understanding, this is required by Qatari Labor Law. However, my written requests on November 1, 2009, and November 25, 2009, to Mr. Hamad al-Attiyah went unanswered. On December 6, 2009, I sent him a registered letter requesting he comply with Qatari Labor Law and provide my end-of-service calculations. I informed him that if I did not receive a response, I would be forced to file a complaint with the Labor Board.

On December 12, 2009, I did file a complaint with the Labor Department. On December 16, 2009, four days later, the company filed a civil complaint against me, seeking 50 million riyal ($13.65 million) for mismanagement. And so my legal troubles in Qatar formally began.

Chapter 8: Banned from Leaving

The al-Attiyahs made sure I would not be allowed to leave because I was under their sponsorship, and they refused to give me an exit permit. To add insult to injury, by filing a frivolous civil action against me, they were able to get the court to impose a travel ban. I would need to post a bond for the 50 million riyals or find a local Qatari to guarantee this amount for me to leave the country. Khalid was well aware of this fact when he put this inflated value on the civil lawsuit.

They also refused to give me a release so I could seek employment in Qatar while my case was working its way through the Qatari legal system. I began to suspect this was the doing of Khalid al-Attiyah, former chairman of Qatar's Human Rights Committee, although I had no proof to back my claim. Unfortunately, this type of irony and injustice are never brought to light, despite Qatar's growing role in the international arena.

There I was, stuck with my family in Doha, unable to leave and unable to work. I hadn't received a salary since May 2009—about seven months. To make matters worse, I was still residing in the company's accommodations, and I was not sure how long it would be until they threw me out on the street.

I decided to send Maysa and the children to Beirut for their Christmas break to get them out of harm's way and give myself time to try to gain a better understanding of what I was in for.

In November 2009, I went to the U.S. Embassy in Doha to inform them of my situation and ask for their assistance in getting out of Qatar. I thought that, with my previous position, all that I had accomplished, and the connections I had, I would be able to find a quick solution. My first meeting at the Embassy was with Maha Dagistani in the consular section for U.S. citizen services. Maha was very friendly and I sensed that she was genuinely concerned; however, I also sensed immediately that she would be of no help: she informed me that my plight was not unusual in Qatar and that the State Department website cautions Americans coming to work in Qatar about their repressive labor regulations.

Indeed, Maha also told me that this was a legal matter and the Embassy could not get involved, and further, that I was not the only American in this situation. She informed me that I needed to hire a local lawyer to defend me and gave me a list of local attorneys that the embassy had compiled. The first name on it was Khalid al-Attiyah, my captor.

I left the embassy feeling hollow. My country, the self-declared "sole super power" that was backing Qatar literally to the hilt, would not or could not even help me. And this is the princedom we protect with the largest U.S. military base outside of the continental United States?

I called a few of the names on the list. I met with some of the lawyers, but it was apparent that many of them were hesitant to take a case against a colleague and sitting government minister.

I called a friend who was a lawyer with a British firm in Qatar. I had met him when he came to Detroit years earlier as part of a delegation from Qatar Petroleum to see if they could attract manufacturing to Qatar. At that time, he was working as a lawyer for Qatar Petroleum. I also found out that his wife was a Beydoun, not a direct relative, but the same family name nonetheless.

I told him my fears and explained my situation. He told me that, in general, the Qatari legal system was uncorrupted, and cases would be judged on their merits. He recommended that I contact Mohsen Makki, a Qatari lawyer who worked with a Lebanese lawyer known for his honesty and ethical behavior. I called Mohsen's office to meet with him and found out he was performing the Hajj pilgrimage. He would be back in two weeks.

While I waited for him to return, I was in a fog, unsure of anything. I didn't know if I would be arrested, what Wataniya was accusing me of, or how I would make a living and support my family. In talking to friends, I was told that legal matters in Qatar take time and that I should try and see if I could resolve my issues with the al-Attiyahs in an amicable way, outside of the courts.

I spoke to people who I had thought were my friends and asked them to assist, but many declined to get involved. They were hesitant to upset the al-Attiyahs. Most said that Khalid al-Attiyah was fair and reasonable and that I should go to him and try and resolve my issue. Also, because the accusations against me were coming from the al-Attiyahs, primarily Khalid himself and his cousin Hamad, most people presumed that indeed I must have embezzled from the company. So I suddenly learned that my credibility was solid only among very few individuals. Everyone else jumped ship and stayed clear. Nobody wanted to get involved; no one wanted to rock their own boats.

People who used to call me all the time and with whom I had spent a considerable amount of time socially faded away. Many stopped answering my calls. And as for the local Qataris I had befriended, I realized that even if they didn't like each other, they rarely sided with a foreigner against a Qatari. And then, Khalid was minister; no one wanted to upset him.

When Mohsen returned from Hajj, I called and scheduled a meeting with him. What a relief—I immediately felt comfortable with him. You could sense that he was a man of integrity and was incorruptible.

I explained my situation and he reaffirmed that the courts in Qatar were fair; however, the process takes time, and time plays into the locals' hands. He sensed my concern and my fear, and his demeanor was comforting. I don't even know if he believed I was innocent; everyone claims that they are innocent. But he took me at face value, and over time, as events unfolded and he saw firsthand how I was being wronged, it strengthened his resolve to exonerate me.

Early in our conversation, he informed me that we needed to pursue the labor claim. Since I had not been served yet in Wataniya's civil case and the company was refusing to grant me an exit permit, I needed to file my labor claim.

We discussed his legal fee. Lawyers in Qatar typically charge a percentage of the claim, about two percent. In my case, that would have been two percent of 50 million riyal, or one million riyal (approximately $300,000). Mohsen, with a warm smile, informed me that this was the customary fee but that because of my situation, he would charge 100,000 QR ($27,400) for the civil case and 30,000 ($8,200) for the labor case. He also allowed me to pay these fees in tranches throughout the duration of the legal proceedings. We often make fun of attorneys and make them the butt of our jokes, but this man was one of the most decent people I have ever met. It felt as though fate had intervened, and I got a man of extremely high moral caliber for this case.

I naturally engaged his services and gave him the agreed-upon retainer. With that, my experience with the Qatari legal system officially began.

The first thing Mohsen asked me to do was to compile all my documents. Of course, I was far along in that process since my last days at Wataniya. I had no idea what the al-Attiyahs had in store for me, so I had gathered as many documents as I could. When I found out what the accusations were, I already held most of the documents that disproved their accusations. And any documents that I did not have, I was able to obtain from my sources inside the company.

Thus after several preparatory meetings with Mohsen, on December 10, 2009, I filed a complaint with Qatar's Department of Labor. The claim contained three items: I had not received my salary and expenses since May 2009; the company was refusing to provide me my end-of-service benefits as prescribed by Qatari law; and the company was denying me an exit permit.

Qatari Labor law is very specific on timelines and remedies. Khalid al-Attiyah knew that the only way to stop the labor department's remedy for nonpayment of salary was to file a civil claim against me. On December 16, 2009, his law firm filed a civil lawsuit against me. I found this out when I went to follow up on my legal claim at the Labor Department—they informed me that they were closing the file because it was now a matter for the courts to decide.

Now I knew that their civil case was filed, but I still did not know what the accusations were, as I hadn't yet been served. I met with Mohsen to get an understanding of how the process works, and he informed me that it could take months for them to serve me. I decided to track down the lawsuit, since time was against me. Every day I spent in Qatar, unable to work, would be detrimental to me and my family, and would be and a win for my captors.

I went down to the Court of First Instance in Dafna and met a lawyer from Mohsen's office. The court is a one of the first towers built in the Dafna, which is the part of Doha that today defines the skyline. Dafna means reclaimed, and the area is all land-fill reclaimed from the sea.

Together we went from office to office, floor to floor, trying to track down the lawsuit. I am probably one of very few individuals who actively set about trying to get served. After several hours, we were able to find the lawsuit, and I accepted service. The documents numbered around 1,000 pages. The lawsuit itself was in Arabic, yet all the exhibits were in English and were documents I was familiar with. I asked Adel to read the document in Arabic so I could ascertain the accusations. I finally knew what the company was accusing me of.

In their initial filing of the frivolous 50 million riyal ($13.65 million) mismanagement lawsuit, the company accused me of embezzling money, self-dealing and dishonesty.

After Adel finished reading the accusations to me, I told him that I had all the documents to prove these allegations were false. Further, every contract and issued payment in question had been authorized by the board.

Adel suggested that I meet with Mohsen and discuss it with him. In the meantime, I had the Arabic documents translated into English so I could have detailed knowledge of their contents. Prior to sitting with Mohsen, I also compiled all the relevant documents on my end.

Mohsen too noticed right off that all the supporting exhibits were in English. Mohsen deduced that this was done to buy time, because as Khalid and his lawyers would have been well aware, Qatari law requires that all documents submitted to the court be in Arabic. Otherwise, the court would require them to be translated into Arabic.

I went through the charges with Mohsen and presented him the supporting documents to support my case. He told me that I would win this case, but it would take time. He even went as far as to say that they didn't have a case—they were just trying to stall and see how long I could hold out. In the meantime, he said we needed to file our labor lawsuit to protect my interests and receive what was rightfully mine. Seeing no other way to reason with these people and resolve this in an amicable manner, I agreed.

Unfortunately for me, the board was comprised of people who were related to government officials and/or the royal family. This was going to be a long and difficult process. I started 2010 with two lawsuits in Qatari courts and a travel ban firmly in place. Also, because Wataniya and the al-Attiyahs had still refused to grant me a work release, I was unable to legally work in Qatar.

Winston Churchill once said, "If you are going through hell, keep going." This was hell, but for the sake of my family, my reputation and my sanity, I needed to keep going. Not only did I decide to keep going, I vowed to fight and to win, for this was personal now. Hamad and his cohorts were waging a campaign in Doha to destroy my reputation and paint all of Wataniya's problems as results of my misjudgment or dishonesty.

At this time, Maysa and the kids were still in Beirut for Christmas break. I had to ensure that our living situation was secure. I went to see the manager of the apartment building we were living in. He had witnessed the effort I had put into the company and was one of the first people I befriended in Doha.

I explained my plight and told him I was worried that Wataniya would try to evict me. He told me as long as I had a case in court, there was little they could do. He told me not to worry, to bring my family back and he would do what he could to protect us. He was true to his word: he protected us and allowed us to stay for ten months without having to pay rent, and he didn't allow Wataniya the opportunity to evict us.

I also needed to ensure the children's school situation was in order. I had enrolled Aya and Jana at the American School in Doha when they had arrived in Qatar the preceding school year. It was one of the best schools in the country and had a magnificent campus. Getting them admitted was a complex process, due to the limited space available, and admissions were difficult. Wataniya was responsible for their tuition per my contract, and they had paid the first year, but then failed to pay the tuition for the 2009/2010 school year. I was in no position to pay, so I went to see the school director and explained my situation. He was sympathetic and told me he would allow the children to finish the school year; I could pay the tuition once I settled my legal issues.

Now that our domicile and the school issue were settled, I called Maysa in Beirut and told her they could come back. I explained that this was going to take time and that we needed to be patient and stay strong.

I have to admit that, at times, I found her stronger than I was. I don't think I could have made it without her love and support. So on January 2, 2010, Maysa and the children returned to Doha. Together, we vowed to fight this. We agreed that we needed to shelter the children from all that was going on and ensure that their lives stayed as normal as possible, while our lives were turning upside down.

On January 3, 2010, the first hearing was held in the civil case filed against me by Wataniya. I met Mohsen and Adel at the courthouse and we went into the courtroom assigned to our case. The room was full of people who were also suing or being sued. Civil cases in Qatar have no trial by jury, just a panel of three judges presided over by a head judge. Since there are not enough Qataris to fill the many positions required, most of the judges are foreign, predominantly Egyptian. In my case, all the head judges and one other were Egyptian, and the other was a Qatari.

There is no case evaluation prior; you just have to go through the process to prove yourself innocent. So when our case was called, Mohsen petitioned the court to translate the more-than-1,000 pages of documents from English to Arabic, noting that otherwise they were inadmissible in the Qatari court system. To translate those documents into Arabic was going to cost the Khalid al-Attiyahs' side a fortune, but it did buy them time. The court ruled in our favor and set the next hearing for February 28, 2010.

After the hearing I conferred with Mohsen regarding removing the travel ban. He told me it was virtually impossible without having a local guarantor for the amount of the lawsuit. He recommended that we obtain the court order and supporting documents that had been submitted to the judge and that the judge based his decision on. Once again, Adel and I went searching for the documents at the court. It took several weeks to find the person who had the documents and the case number. After we obtained that information, we were informed that the file was misplaced and they would have to look for it. Faced with a dead-end, Mohsen focused on my labor lawsuit against Wataniya.

In mid January 2010, we filed our lawsuit against the company seeking back pay, expenses and end-of-service benefits. After the labor lawsuit was submitted, our first hearing was scheduled for February 10, 2010. Labor cases are usually fast-tracked through the court system.

CRIMINAL CHARGES

On Thursday, February 4, 2010, I received a call from the Qatari police department informing me that Wataniya had filed a criminal complaint against me for embezzlement and that I was to report immediately to the Khalifa Police Station. I called Mohsen and asked what I should do. He said that I had to go or they would come and arrest me. He suggested that I wait until Sunday, because the weekend in Qatar falls on Friday and Saturday. If I went in on a Thursday, they would keep me over the weekend.

I was a complete wreck. Maysa, my cousin, a family friend and I spent the weekend together, worried over this new development. I contacted Maha at the U.S. Embassy and informed her about the situation. She told me to go, and that if anything should happen, to have someone contact her, and the consular section would send someone to visit me in jail. It wasn't very reassuring.

I prepared my documents and Sunday morning, my cousin Aboudi and I reported to the police station. Entering the police station that day, I had never felt so helpless. In my entire life, I had never been in trouble with the law nor had the police ever questioned me. This was the most humiliating moment of my life, to date. I knew I had done nothing wrong, but I was in a foreign country. I couldn't stop thinking that this was going to be a kangaroo court.

We walked into the station and I went to the desk officer and informed him that I had received a call to report to the station for questioning. He asked me for my name and Qatari ID number. After looking into the logbook for my name, he told me that I needed to see the officer in the evening. He told me to go and come back that night.

That evening, around 8:00 p.m. Aboudi and I returned to the police station. Again, I approached the desk officer and informed him that I was summoned to appear. He searched the logbook and said, "Are you the American?"

I nodded yes and he told me to take a seat. He went to the officer on duty's office and I could hear him tell the officer that the American from Wataniya was here.

Still, Aboudi and I had to sit there for about three hours before the officer came out of his office. Instead of coming to me, though, he went to one of his subordinates and told him to question me. For whatever reason, it seems he had to leave and would be back. The young officer came out and called me into his office.

I went in with my paperwork and asked why I had been called in to the police station. He told me that my company had filed a complaint that I had embezzled company funds.

After I asked in what way, he explained that I had raised my own salary without the approval of the board, that I had taken a housing allowance when the company provided me housing, and that I had taken a car allowance when I had a company car. He also stated that I was accused of depositing profits from the Ghia holdings, the company's Lebanese operations company, into my personal account in Lebanon.

I inquired whether the company had presented any evidence to substantiate its charges, and he informed me that they had not. They filed the charges with no backup.

Since I had all my documents with me, I began going through everything that showed all the charges were baseless.

He took my statement and asked me to go and translate the documents in English to Arabic and bring them back. I told him it would take a few days, and he said that wouldn't be a problem; just to bring them when they were done.

After he finished taking my statement, he proceeded to the officer's office and told him he thought there was no basis for the company's allegations.

The officer told him to file his report and, once I submitted the translations, to forward his recommendations to the prosecutor general's office. For now, I was free to go.

I left around 1:00 in the morning, totally exhausted, but happy at the outcome. I returned a few days later with the translated documents and I asked the young officer what came next.

He said since there was no truth to the allegations, the file would be closed and the charges dismissed. I was overjoyed. I thought that would be the last I would have to deal with the criminal issue.

That issue having been put to bed, I focused on the remaining lawsuits. That Wednesday, February 10, 2010, I went to the court to attend the first hearing for the labor lawsuit. Mohsen told me that most likely the company's lawyer would not attend, because they had until the third hearing to show up before being declared in default. As he had projected, the company did not show, and another hearing was scheduled for February 23, 2010.

On the 23rd I went to court again for my labor hearing, and Wataniya's lawyers again did not show. The court set the third hearing for March 2, 2010, when Wataniya would have to show up. In the meantime, they had succeeded in fraying our nerves and delaying the proceedings by one month.

February 28, 2010 was our second hearing in the civil case. Wataniya submitted the translated documents to the court. However, they had reduced the documents by about 80%. The court set the next hearing date for March 23, 2010. That was when I would have to submit my rebuttal.

After court, Mohsen gave me the newly selected documents and instructed me to go through and put together my response, and then we would meet to discuss. So I went through the documents with a fine-toothed comb. I had reviewed the documents over and over to ensure that I did not overlook anything.

If this had happened in any country other than Qatar, the charges would have been laughable, but these people knew what they were doing. Their intention from the beginning was to hold me in Qatar and throw all the accusations they could at me to force me to negotiate a monetary settlement that would allow me to leave. What they didn't count on was that I had compiled a library of documents that would render their allegations baseless.

In that region, with their political influence, the al-Attiyahs could influence any gray areas to be decided in their favor. But there was little they could do if something was black and white. Their accusations and my responses were just that: black and white.

I went about selecting the necessary documents and having those in English translated to Arabic. I wrote the response in English for Mohsen, and then I asked my maternal uncle in Lebanon to translate it into Arabic.

My uncle was a sociology professor at the Lebanese University in Beirut and an eminent political strategist. He received his PhD from the Sorbonne in Paris. His spoke both Arabic and French like a native, and he authored many books in both languages. He taught himself English, and his translations were the only ones I truly trusted, because he knew my future hung in the balance. He would go on to translate most of the critical documents I needed, for free.

On March 2, 2010, the third hearing in the labor case was held, and Wataniya's lawyers finally attended. For the first time, the case was moving forward. The court gave them until March 9 to respond to my allegations.

On March 7, I went to the Human Rights Department of the Minister of Interior to have my sponsor switched from Wataniya to another company, thus enabling me to find a job while I pursed my legal challenges. I submitted a written explanation of my situation. They logged my complaint and told me to check with them in a few weeks.

On March 9, Wataniya submitted their response in the Labor case, which was basically a carbon copy of the allegations they had made in the civil case. The Labor Court took the matter under advisement and set the next hearing for March 31.

HUMAN RIGHTS DEPARTMENT

I spent the majority of the month preparing for my hearing on March 23. I assembled the entire document—it was translated, cataloged and bound perfectly. I met with Mohsen and presented the complete package to him. The depth of my supporting documents impressed him. In the document, I tackled all the accusations with thoroughness and did not leave anything to the imagination. It was obvious that I hadn't done anything wrong or acted without Wataniya's permission.

On March 23rd we presented our documents to the court, which subsequently set a hearing for May 10 when Wataniya was to respond to submission.

On the March 31st labor hearing, the court appointed an expert to assess the documents and submit his findings to the court. The next hearing would be May 12.

On April 5th I went to the Human Rights department to check on the status of my petition for transfer of sponsorship. They told me that they needed a copy of the court expert's report to proceed. I asked how I was supposed to support my family when I could not leave the country or work, but their only answer was that this was the process.

As all these legal proceedings were ongoing, Maysa and I still had to maintain a semblance of normality at home for the sake of the children. Aya and Jana were still attending school. We kept them busy with after school activities, and three days a week we had a tutor come to the house to teach them Arabic. As for Maysa's and my social life, many of our friends in Doha had stopped calling or inviting us to events.

I don't believe people were being malicious; expatriates in Qatar live in constant fear of falling out of favor with their local sponsors or alienating some powerful Qatari.

We had no Qatari friends; the Qataris I knew were business associates. If they needed you, they called. Our circle of friends dwindled to just a handful. We spent most our time with friends who lived in the same apartment complex that we did. When Maysa and kids eventually moved back to the States, some of those friends became my only local moral support.

There were other friends whom we would get together with on occasion, but the friends in our apartment complex were family. We would see each other almost on a daily basis, either in each other's apartments or during potluck dinners. They were genuinely concerned and tried to make us feel like we were not alone. They helped cushion us from our anguish.

During the time Maysa and children were there, life in Qatar was bearable. Doha is a small city, with relatively little to do for recreation. Even if you are working full time, after a month or two you get on plane for Dubai or Beirut to regain your sanity. And prior to my "problem," that is what we did. We took every opportunity we could to go Lebanon. Both Maysa and I have family there, and at times, my parents or hers would be in Lebanon and we would go visit them. The best part of living in Doha is that you are in close proximity (by plane) to some great destinations. But being stuck in Doha is unbearable.

During the school days we did little except spend time together as a family; we stayed at home for the most part, and with our friends at the apartment complex. It seemed like we always had someone over for dinner. Maysa and I would work out when we could; it was important for us to stay in physical as well as mental shape.

Maysa and I vowed not to let these people beat us. We would not get depressed. We took it day by day and used the time to get closer as a family. I would take Jamal swimming when he wanted or just spend time with him in the apartment. I really enjoyed watching him develop.

It was my longing to be with him, Aya and Jana that got me through from the time they left until the time we were reunited, one year later.

On the weekends we did what everyone in Qatar does: go to one of the malls. Strolling outdoors is out of the question, given the heat. We would do our grocery shopping, grab a bite to eat and sometimes see a movie. On occasion, we would go out to Sealine for a picnic on the beach. The kids kept busy with their friends at school, with play dates or birthdays. Maysa was very good at arranging activities for them.

On April 27, 2010, my attorney arranged a meeting with the court-appointed expert to discuss the case. He had previously met with Wataniya's attorney, and they presented their argument as to why I shouldn't be entitled to my salary and benefits. Their argument was in line with the civil case accusations: that I had raised my own salary, took housing and car allowances I wasn't entitled to, and deposited company funds in my personal account.

The court expert was an Egyptian named Khalid Asker. Everything I had heard about him was that he was fair and God fearing. He could not be bought, and he was thorough. When I sat down with him, I sensed that he was buying Wataniya's story. His tone, at the beginning of the meeting, was accusatory and short. After he went through the reasons Wataniya had given him as to why I not entitled to my funds, it was our turn to respond. Mohsen and I went through each point, one by one. Where the company had only made unsubstantiated allegations, we presented documented proof supporting our position. You didn't need to be an expert to figure out who was lying and who was telling the truth. By the time we had finished the meeting, his demeanor was totally different. I sensed that we had prevailed and won him over to our side. It is very hard to skew documented facts, and the facts supported our position.

In the meantime, I had been working to get the U.S. Embassy involved in my case. Maha had turned over my file to the counselor in charge, Alex Ave-Lallemant, counselor section chief.

May 10 was the civil hearing at which Wataniya was supposed to respond to our answer to their allegations. Instead of responding to our answer and the documents we presented that totally negated their first set of accusations, they proceeded to submit additional documentation, trying to add credibility to their lawsuit. In fact, they submitted a new set of addendums, the bulk of them in English, without providing the required translation. It was blatantly obvious that they were just prolonging the proceedings, and they had no case. The court set the next appointment for us to respond on June 28. Once again, Mohsen gave me the documents and asked me to review them and put together the rebuttal with supporting documents.

The May 12 labor hearing came, but Khalid Asker, the court expert, did not submit his findings to the court. A new hearing was scheduled for May 27. Adel, the Egyptian attorney who worked with Mohsen, was able to obtain a copy of Asker's labor report. He called me and told me to come to the courthouse, but wouldn't tell me why. Since I lived about two miles from the court, I was there in ten minutes.

When I got there, he was standing outside with a smile on his face. How he got the report I don't know, but most of the court staff were Egyptian and he must have used his personal ties to obtain the copy. The report was in Arabic, and since I could not read Arabic and it was about 200 pages, I asked him to cut to the chase and give me the results.

He told me that Asker's report had come in in my favor, and that his recommendation was that I was owed 800,000 riyals ($220,000). Even more important, the report negated the allegations in Wataniya's civil case. I felt vindicated at last and felt that this might come to an end soon.

I hugged and kissed Adel and went home to tell Maysa. That evening we had dinner with all our friends and I told them the great news. There was a sense of euphoria. I went the next day to the Human Rights Department and submitted the report per their request. I thought for sure they would give me the release.

The next day, on the 27th of May at the labor hearing, the report was officially submitted. Wataniya's lawyer didn't even bother to show up, probably because he had already obtained a copy. The court scheduled another hearing for June 27.

On May 31st I again went to the Human Rights Department to check on my release. To my amazement, I was informed that my request had been denied. I was livid. I asked why, but they wouldn't give me a reason; they just told me it was denied.

I demanded to see the officer in charge and sat in front of his office and waited about two hours until he would see me.

When I was finally able to explain my entire situation to him, he seemed to sympathize and told me to submit a letter requesting an appeal.

That night, I met with Mohsen and he helped me draft the appeal in Arabic. On June 2, I went back and submitted the documents. He told me once the court issued its verdict, to bring him a copy.

June was a busy month, with the school year coming to an end. Our financial situation was becoming tight; we were living off our savings.

At the end of the school year, Doha generally starts to empty out. Most of the expatriate families begin to leave. Most senior workers have a month vacation during the summer, but the families tend to go back home first, with the dads following. Most executives are entitled to an annual airline ticket for themselves and their families. During July and August, Doha really becomes a ghost town. Even the Qataris leave for Europe, the U.S. or Lebanon. The only ones left behind are the laborers and those who just can't leave.

Ironically, this was my favorite time in Doha. The city was tranquil, the traffic jams were gone, and everything moved at a slower pace. However, the heat was unbearable, reaching 120°–130° F. Maysa and I were hoping that I would be able to lift my travel ban before the court's summer recess. But the funny thing is, even without the travel ban, I still needed an exit permit from Wataniya because I was technically still under their sponsorship. At the time, I was in Qatar illegally because my residence permit had expired in April.

Wataniya's HR director also contacted me around that time and told me that they wanted to renew my permit. She asked if I would give her my passport. I refused.

On June 26, 2010, the labor court came back with a verdict in my favor and awarded me 621,000 riyals ($170,000), totally vindicating my position. Maysa and I were thrilled with the victory, but Wataniya was sure to appeal the verdict. In the meantime, Mohsen informed me that with the judgment, we could begin to garnish the company's assets. On June 28th we submitted our responses in the civil case and the court set the next hearing for November 7th, after the summer recess.

On July 17th we had our first garnishment hearing. Mohsen told me not much would happen during the hearing. He was right—the court just scheduled another hearing for September 21st.

Our next civil hearing was scheduled for November 7, 2010. By this time, most of our friends had left. School was out, and I asked Maysa if she wanted to go back to the U.S. She was adamant that she didn't want to leave me, so we stayed together, trying to keep the family busy and enjoying our time together.

In July, my parents came to visit. They had been in Lebanon, spending their summer as they usually do, and were deeply concerned about my situation. We thought if they came and saw that we were all right, it would put their minds at ease. They came and stayed for about two weeks.

I would go, from time to time, to the Human Rights Department to follow up on my sponsorship transfer. In August, Mohsen went to the U.S. on vacation for a month. My parents went back to Lebanon and we were left alone in Qatar.

Finally in late August, the Human Rights Department notified me that they had approved my transfer of sponsorship and that they had sent the recommendation to the Minister of Interior for his approval and signature. It seems that the transfer of sponsorship without the approval of the previous sponsor required the Minister's approval. I felt that this might be a problem, because the Minister of the Interior, Sheikh Abdullah Bin Khalid al-Thani (a close relative of the Emir and the prime minister, of course), was known for his support of radical Islamic causes. He was only kept in that position to protect him from international persecution. The Minister of State for Internal Affairs, Sheikh Abdulla Bin Nasser Bin Khalifa al-Thani, handled the day-to-day affairs of the ministry. Sheikh Abdulla bin Nasser was the nephew of Hamad al-Attiyah, one of my nemeses.

However, on August 25th I was pleasantly surprised when I went to the Human Rights Department. They confirmed that my transfer was approved and that I could go to the Residency Permits Department and transfer my sponsorship.

Now I needed to find a sponsor. A friend of my friend Ahmed, who owned a printing company and worked for the landlord of one of our locations, agreed to sponsor me. Ahmed and I had become friends during the time I worked for Wataniya. He was well aware of my plight and was put off by the treatment I was subjected to by Wataniya. He was one of those people who didn't have to help; he had nothing to gain and much to lose. But his sense of justice made him want to help.

He and I spent days going through the bureaucracy to transfer my sponsorship. He took time out of his busy schedule, and finally after three or four days, we succeeded and I was no longer under Wataniya's sponsorship. Making a difficult business worse was the fact that we were trying to accomplish this task during Ramadan, when most government offices were operating at reduced hours.

During Ramadan, people in the Gulf seem to put their lives on hold. Ramadan is supposed to be a time of introspection. Muslims are required to fast from food, water, and sex from dawn to dusk. It is a time for family, reflection and charity. However, in the Gulf they merely changed their days to nights and nights to day. They would sleep all day and stay up all night. Instead of eating less to sense the hunger of the destitute, they ate more. They threw away enough food to feed a multitude of hungry people. They came to work with an attitude that they were doing the world a favor by fasting.

For Muslims in the West, fasting is more in line with the meaning of Ramadan. People there don't have the luxury of not working or changing their schedules to accommodate the occasion. I remember my father going to work at Ford at 5:00 a.m. and not eating or drinking until it was time to break his fast at sundown. And when Ramadan happened to fall in the summer months, that could be 9:00 or 10:00 p.m. This was faith and the true meaning of sacrifice.

Chapter 9: Life in Qatar and the Never-ending Attempts to Remove the Travel Ban

During the summer of 2010, with the courts closed for the summer recess and Doha mostly empty, I got a call from a local Qatari who owned an events management company. They were putting on the "Made in America" show to highlight American companies that want to do business in Qatar. We had worked together the previous year when he put on his first show, and I took a booth to display our U.S. brands, Caribou Coffee, Sbarro and Rainforest Café.

He had asked me to help him organize the show, in fact. Ahmad Chebbani, the chairman of the American Arab Chamber of Commerce, had suggested that he contact me because I was in Qatar and had experience with this type of event when I was with the Chamber. I had to decline because I was busy with Wataniya, and under Qatari Labor law moonlighting for someone else could cause your residence permit to be revoked, or worse, your sponsor can throw you in jail. And even though he had the support of the commercial section of the U.S. Embassy, the first show was not successful.

Despite this, I had been working with Rashid since January in an unofficial advisory role and as a part-time consultant. I was careful not to make my participation known, because if the al-Attiyahs became aware, they would have most definitely had me thrown in jail for working illegally.

Rashid asked me to take charge of the show and help him put on the event. Now that I had switched my sponsorship and could legally work in Qatar, I took on the assignment, happy to know I had employment for a couple of months. The show was scheduled for October 12-15, 2010.

In July, Maysa had started working for our friend Abe Madi at Jefferson Contracting, his construction company. Abe had landed a new contract at the New Doha Airport and he was ramping up his staff. He asked Maysa to assist him, and so we had some income coming in.

As the summer of 2010 was coming to a close, people were starting to return. As the school year was starting soon, we needed to have a talk with the people at the American School Doha. The administrator, by that time, had left, and a new one had taken his place. Maysa and I met with her in mid August to see if they were going to allow the children to attend that school year, since the past year's tuition was still unpaid.

The new administrator took the matter to the school board and they denied our request to allow them to attend until I settled my legal matters. I understood their position, but it was a dramatic turn of events. Maysa and I didn't know what to do. The best option would be for them to go back to Michigan, where we still had our home and they could attend public school, but Maysa was adamant that she would not leave me alone in Qatar under the circumstances.

Her job paid our living expenses while we had no rent payment—we were basically squatting in the Wataniya accommodations. We decided that I should look for employment. Even though I was still preparing for the "Made in the USA" Show, the income derived from it was minimal and it appeared that Rashid was not willing to invest the proper capital for a show of this magnitude. In addition, he had a partner and childhood friend, a Palestinian who was raised in Qatar, who didn't want me in the picture and did everything to move me aside; I eventually stepped aside and let him take over.

I started to contact people I had known or met to see if they had any openings or knew of any possible employment. Even with my resume, no one was willing to publicly hire me. They were afraid of the al-Attiyahs and did not want to aggravate them. I did get a lot of sympathetic rejections.

September 2010 was very difficult. We didn't have a school lined up; and then a new building manager took over at the apartment complex.

It became clear that I would probably have to move out. However, renting a family accommodation in Doha in a decent compound or building was expensive. Since we were already paying a mortgage on an empty house in Michigan, it was too much to bear. To make matters worse, the new building manager was putting pressure on us to get out. On several occasions she would have maintenance turn off the electricity to the unit and tell us it was the electrical company. However, I had friends in the maintenance department and they would turn it back on. No electricity means no air conditioning, and the outside temperature was hovering around 120ºF.

Towards the beginning of October, I decided to send the family back to Michigan. Maysa still objected, but I felt things were going to get worse. They were scheduled to leave on October 9, 2010.

I had to be out of the apartment by October 11, so I set out to find a place to stay. I had been looking and putting out feelers for a place, but most of them wanted a year's lease and postdated checks to cover future months. And that was for tiny, dark apartments where I felt I would suffocate or get depressed.

By luck, a friend of mine from the apartment complex found out that a friend of his, prior to the real estate crash of 2008, had bought two apartments on The Pearl.

The Peal-Qatar is situated in the bay near the West Bay Lagoon Area of Doha. The island development is shaped like a string of pearls and diamonds. This offshore manmade island was to include 21 residential towers and 410 villas, 3 luxury hotels, 3 marinas, and other facilities for retail, entertainment, dining, and education. Most of the promised projects never materialized. Out of the 21 residential towers, only a handful were completed and turned over to the buyers.

One of his units was in a three-tower project, one of the few completed. Since he had to take possession of the unit, I worked out a deal where I would lease it from him for three months and furnish it with what we had accumulated during our time in Doha. In return, he would give me a reduced rent and waive the deposit. It was a small two-bedroom apartment on the 9th floor with a nice view of the marina and the bay. It made my solitude a little more bearable.

This apartment on the Pearl Island ended up becoming my refuge while I was held in Qatar. Although Qatar is a peninsula, my home was this island. I took solace that when I was home, I was not technically in Qatar. Even though I was connected to Doha by a quarter-mile-long bridge, while on the island, I was physically and mentally outside of Qatar.

When it became clear that leaving Qatar was impossible, I only ventured onto the mainland for shopping, meetings with my attorney, court hearings and an occasional meeting. Any of my friends who wanted to see me had to come to the island. And after I sold my car in April 2011, I ventured off the island even more rarely.

October 25th was Aya's 10th birthday. She was already back home in Michigan by then, trying to learn a new routine. I sent her a bouquet of flowers and Maysa threw her a beautiful belly dancing themed party. I called her to wish her a happy birthday.

Aya is a lot like me—she rarely shows her emotions—but during our conversation, she began to cry. She told me all she wanted was that I come home. I had never missed one of my children's birthdays, but that year I missed her birthday and Jana's 8th birthday. I put down the phone and cried. I had hit a new low.

U.S. EMBASSY

The embassy was still giving me the same answer: this was a legal matter and they couldn't get involved. From my initial meeting with Maha, I received comforting words but no real action. Early on, and several times, I requested to meet with Ambassador Joseph La Baron. But there I was, a U.S. citizen, being held a virtual hostage in a foreign country, and my own ambassador refused to meet with me. What exactly is America's relationship with Qatar?

Maha contacted Alex Ave-Lallemant, Consular Section Chief at the U.S. Embassy, but his assistance was minimal. In December 2009, early on in my ordeal, I met with Dao Le, Senior Commercial Officer at the U.S. Embassy, at the Four Seasons in Doha. At the time, I was wondering why I was meeting with the commercial officer. When I inquired, Dao informed me that the Ambassador had asked him to meet with me, because he was under the impression that this was a contract issue that would be best handled by the Commercial Desk.

I sat with Dao and explained my situation. He recommended that I send a letter to Khalid al-Attiyah and try and resolve this issue amicably. I took his advice, and on December 24, 2009, I sent an email to Khalid requesting a meeting to try and resolve our issues. He did not respond directly.

A few days later I got a call from a lawyer working for him. He informed me that he was calling on behalf of Khalid and that if he wanted meet, I could come see him and discuss the issue. I had known this lawyer since I started with Wataniya. When we needed something from Khalid or his law firm, I would contact him. I thought this was a positive sign and hoped that this might resolve things.

I asked Mohsen, my attorney, to accompany me to the meeting. At the meeting, another of Khalid's attorneys who handled his business affairs was present. The meeting didn't last long; it quickly degenerated into accusations and threats on their part. We left the meeting knowing that there was only a legal remedy. As we were leaving, Khalid's lawyer told us he knew that 50 million riyals ($12.7 million) was an exaggerated number, but he could get the board to accept a settlement of 10 million riyals ($3.4 million) to let me go. Their game was basic extortion; pay us and take the blame or we will hold you hostage for a long time.

Finally, after exhausting all my options, in late June 2010, I contacted Ed Begale, vice chancellor at the University of Michigan-Dearborn. Ed and I were good friends and Maysa and I were friends with his wife, Gail, as well. Ed was very active in the Michigan political scene and the Michigan Democratic Party and was basically the state lobbyist for the University of Michigan. He had started his career working for the Levins, Senator Carl Levin and his brother, Congressman Sander Levin. I asked Ed to connect me with someone in Senator Levin's office.

Senator Levin was the senior senator from Michigan, my home state, and chairman of the Armed Services Committee. With such a large U.S. military presence in Qatar, I figured he should have some clout. Ed came through and put me in contact with Gina Dusseau Sherman. I called Gina and informed her of my situation and told her that I was having a hard time getting an appointment with Ambassador La Baron.

On July 1, 2010, Senator Levin wrote a letter to the Embassy asking that they assist me and arrange a meeting with the Ambassador. Finally on October 14, 2010, the Embassy responded with an email that the Ambassador agreed to meet with me. On November 8, 2010, almost one year after my legal problems started, I got a meeting with the U.S. Ambassador.

But it didn't help much—during the meeting, he basically said there was nothing he could do to assist me.

REMOVING THE TRAVEL BAN

Along with bidding my family goodbye and moving to a new apartment, I had several labor hearings. On October 5th we had a garnishment hearing, and on October 6th we had an appeals hearing. Wataniya had, immediately after I was awarded a judgment, filed an appeal in the labor case verdict. The court ruled again in my favor and the judgment stood. Wataniya had one more appeal, and that was scheduled for November 25th. In the meantime, I was determined to get the travel ban lifted. With the completion of the transfer of sponsorship, I no longer needed an exit permit from Wataniya, but rather from my new sponsor, which would not be a problem.

The court file that was the basis of the ruling in the travel ban was still missing. I made it my mission to find it, and I went to the court in mid October looking for it. For the next several days, I went from office to office in the courthouse. I found the logbook and obtained the file number. We tracked all the files with numbers before mine and after, yet there was no sign of my file.

Finally, one of the Qataris in charge got involved—probably because he was sick of seeing me. He called the person in charge of the files to his office and told him to find my file and bring it to him.

I was astonished that the file turned up. It consisted of the exact same accusations from the civil case and was just as thick, with papers in English. I asked how a ruling could have been made when the documents were all in English. The Qatari at the court told me that the judge probably hadn't read it. The judge probably just signed my travel ban based on the fact that it had come from Khalid al-Attiyah and had such a large sum attached to it.

I took a copy of the file to Mohsen to review. He told me that there were only two ways to remove the travel ban: either put up a bond for the amount of the lawsuit or find a Qatari who would guarantee the outcome of the case.

I didn't have that kind of money and I had few Qatari friends, none of whom would be willing to guarantee $12.7 million, regardless whether the allegations were true or not. No one would take that chance, as al-Attiyah was well aware.

So, even though I had won the labor case and the judgment I received basically negated the civil case, I was still stuck in Qatar. This is a standard practice that gives the local a home-field advantage. During my captivity I heard many horror stories about travel bans placed on foreigners.

My only option was to find a Qatari willing to guarantee my case. My cousin found me one who would do it if I paid him $30,000. I agreed and Mohsen, who had no direct knowledge of any arrangement I might have made with that Qatari, did the necessary paperwork to have him become my guarantor. We submitted the paperwork to a special court for expedited matters, and then we went to see the sitting judge. Typically the judge would have ordered that the local just guarantee that I would come back for the verdict. But this judge told the Qatari who was guaranteeing me that he was going to hold him accountable for any amount of a judg-

ment, also. That didn't matter anyway because, in the end, since my guarantor didn't have a job, the judge denied the request. I was devastated.

On November 7th, we had a civil hearing and were able to respond to
Wataniya's second set of accusations. Once again, we presented all the
documents properly translated that negated, without a doubt, their false
accusations. The next hearing was scheduled for December 27th. On November 25th we had our second (and final) appeals hearing in the labor
case. The court ruled in my favor again and the verdict would become
final in 90 days. Future court hearings in the labor case would focus on
seizing the company's assets until the judgment was satisfied. I could
also put the company's general manager in jail until the judgment had
been satisfied.

That sounded great. But after I left the company, Khalid al-Attiyah
had put his aunt, Nada Fares, in charge as the general manager. She was
Syrian, as was Khalid's mother, but had obtained a Qatari citizenship.
(This is not an easy task.) I heard horror stories about her from the staff.
She never missed an opportunity to try to smear me. She would tell everyone that I had stolen from the company, and she would ask any vendor I dealt with if I had gotten a kickback. She always got the same answer, though—that I had been nothing but professional in my dealings
with them.

If the shoe were on the other foot, she and her nephew wouldn't hesitate to throw me in jail. However, we did not choose to do that; we just
went about trying to collect our money by garnishing their accounts,
seizing their restaurants, and putting a freeze on their commercial regis-
try. During Nada's tenure at Wataniya, the company was stripped of all
its brands and she went on to close over 30 outlets.

I spent most of December trying to find a way to get the travel ban
lifted or, as a worst case scenario, to expedite the civil case. On December
27th, the court appointed a financial expert to review the case and make
his recommendation. I spent that holiday season alone in Doha.

In January I was still trying to figure out a way to get the travel ban
lifted, but needed someone who believed in me enough to guarantee me
with the court. I turned to one of my former employees who was having
financial problems. He was trying to pay off certain bank loans from his
days in Dubai. He had a wife and two young girls, so I worked out an
arrangement for him to sponsor me with the courts. He was well aware
that if the court accepted, he would be unable to travel until the case
was settled. And if, by some fluke, I had a judgment issued against me in
the case, he would be responsible if I didn't pay it. So I worked out a deal

with him and agreed. He felt confident that I would eventually win and that it was only a matter of time. Plus, he had no plans to travel. So we went to Mohsen to prepare the documents. This time we had the added benefit of a final judgment in the labor case.

Once again, we submitted the necessary documentation, and on January 31, 2011, we went to see a judge.

When we got to his office, Adel went in to see him, and then came out a few minutes later and told us he wanted to see my new guarantor. He went in and came out a few minutes later, informing us that the judge had rejected the request. Shocked, I asked Adel if I could go in and see the judge, and he simply motioned that there really wasn't anything I could do.

But my years as a door-to-door canvasser had taught me to never take no for an answer. Plus, I had nothing to lose. I went into the judge's office and humbly asked if I could speak to him. He motioned me in, and I went about explaining my situation. He should have known all this, if he had read the papers; but I informed him the travel ban had been placed without the proper documents, and the amount placed on the civil case was malicious, that it was set at such a high amount simply to ensure no one would guarantee me.

I also told him about the final verdict in my labor case that negated all the accusations in the civil case, and that the plaintiff was stalling to hold me hostage in the country. I explained how my guarantor was willing to put himself in my place, and that would ensure that if by some fluke the company won a judgment, they had recourse against him.

It must have finally struck a chord with him. He told me to call my guarantor back into his office. As he made his way back in, the judge asked him if he knew what he was getting into—that he would not be able to leave the country if I left, and that if the company won a judgment and I didn't settle it, the company could go after him.

He acknowledged that he was aware and proceeded to repeat most of the points in the argument that I had just given. The judge looked at us, smiled, and signed the order lifting the travel ban.

Adel couldn't believe it. We were all ecstatic. We had accomplished something that few had. Once again, the Qatari judiciary system came through. I left the court elated.

I called Maysa at 3:00 a.m. in Michigan to tell her the good news. About three hours later, I received a text message from the Ministry of Interior that my travel ban had been lifted. I thought I would be out of Qatar soon.

Bounced Checks

The next day, I contacted my sponsor and informed him that I had gotten the travel ban lifted. It was time to get my exit permit.

Unfortunately, I should have known it wouldn't turn out to be so easy. That same day, I received a call from the central police station notifying me that I had bounced a check and needed to come down to the station.

I knew it must have been a Wataniya check. Under Qatari law, the person who signs a check bears the responsibility for that check, even if it is a company check and you are no longer an employee.

I had had several such issues. While I was with Wataniya, I would issue post-date checks for rent of employee accommodations or restaurant locations. If one of those checks bounced, the landlord had the option to sue the company in civil court to recoup his money, or he could file a criminal complaint with the police against the person who signed the check. If that person didn't make the check good, he would be charged and thrown in jail. What most people did was pay the check and then file a lawsuit against the company to get their money back. But sometimes people were liable for millions of dollars in checks, and Qatar was a nation that still had a debtor's prison. And to make things worse, if you have a bounced check, an automatic travel ban is placed on you. I was not aware of this until after some of Wataniya's checks bounced, but at that point it was too late. Most of the checks were in the hands of the landlords and I was going to be held accountable, even though I no longer had anything to do with the company.

Well, Elaine, the finance manager, once again came to my rescue.

Since I had left the company, Khalid al-Attiyah had sent a letter to the bank removing me as a signatory on the accounts. So Elaine had begun exchanging the rent checks with new ones, with Nada as the signatory. She did it under the Attiyahs' radar and was able to get most of the checks back. I only had a problem with the landlord of the Wataniya corporate office. He had a check that bounced and ended up taking me to court. But Elaine was able to make the check good and gave me a release, which I submitted to the court, and the case was adjourned.

I had not worked for Wataniya for over a year and yet I was still liable! So this time, when I thought I was about to finally be able to leave Qatar, I sent someone to the police station to see what this was about. I was told to never go yourself, because they could hold you until you made the check good. I sent a Qatari friend who was connected with the police department. He came back and reported that four rent checks had been returned for the villa that was rented for one of the employees, and Nada had refused to honor the checks. The total amount was 48,000 riyals ($12,000). I knew that this matter would have to be taken care of if I wanted to leave Doha, so I contacted the landlord to see if I could work something out.

The landlord was a sheikh from the al-Thani family. The amount was pittance to him, but you would think it was his last dollar. I wasn't even dealing with the sheikh himself; I was going through an Egyptian who handled his affairs and wanted to prove his worth to the sheikh. I tried to reason with him and explain my situation, but he was having nothing to do with it. So in the end, I would have to pay the money if I wanted to lift that travel ban.

I arranged to meet him at the police station. I brought the cash and he brought the checks. I paid him in the presence of the police and obtained a release. Before I left, I asked the officer to see if I had anything on my file that would prevent me from traveling. To my surprise, he informed me that I had two other travel bans related to Wataniya checks.

One was for the landlord, and another was for a check to a Qatari. I told him that I had the release for the first, but did not for the second. He informed me that I would have to call him and he would need to come to the police station to remove the travel ban. In regards to the release, because it was through the court, I just needed to bring the court ruling.

The next day I went to the court and obtained a copy of the ruling and took it down to the police station. With that, the officer removed the first travel ban. With regard to the second, I didn't have any way to contact that man, nor was I even certain whether he would come to the station. I contacted Elaine, who at that time had moved back to Lebanon. I asked her if she had his contact info or if she could get me the file from Wataniya, from one of the girls who were still there. She said she would try.

In the meantime, I started asking around to other people and eventually got his phone number. On February 3, 2011, I called him and explained my situation. He told me that he was outside Doha on the North Coast, but since it was Thursday, he would meet me at the police station on Sunday and take care of it.

He was true to his word; he drove all the way to Doha and met me and signed my release. He had a strong sense of fairness and right and wrong. He did this because it was the right thing to do and he was a fundamentally good person.

All possible obstacles for me leaving Doha were now removed, and on February 7, 2011 at 2:12 p.m., I received another text message: the travel ban had been lifted.

I immediately called my sponsor and asked him to meet me at the passport office at the airport to get me an exit permit. Sure enough, about an hour later, he met me there and we went to obtain my exit permit.

We presented the documentation. The lady studied the papers and her computer, and then told us that the system would not allow her to issue an exit permit. We inquired if there was a travel ban, and she said no. She told us to go back to the central police station to check into the matter. Since the police station was near the passport office, we proceeded there immediately.

The officer in charge looked up my file and told us he didn't see anything. He recommended we go to the other side of the building to see the criminal division. We did, and once again, the officer informed us that he saw nothing in my file. He said to try the passport office again. So we went to the passport office, and once again, we could not get an exit permit. I was beginning to lose hope. No one seemed to have any idea what was going on.

We went back to the central police station. Again, the officer looked up my file; now he told us to go to the police station at al-Rayyan. We immediately proceeded to al-Rayyan, and on our way at 5:17 p.m. I received a text message that a travel ban had been issued by the prosecutor's office. My heart dropped.

I showed the text to my sponsor in disbelief. We reached the al-Rayyan Police station, and at the front desk, we were told to go see the public fraud division. When we got there, we were told that the officer had left and to come back at 8:00 p.m. So we went to my sponsor's office until 8:00 p.m. to wait. I tried to remain hopeful, sure that there must have been some kind of mix up.

At 8:00 p.m. we went back and met with the officer, who told me that I needed to go see the public funds division of the prosecutor's office in the morning.

I was devastated. I called Maysa and told her what had happened. She sensed the despair in my voice and tried to console me, telling me everything would be okay. But this sort of intrigue suggested the strong hand of Khalid al-Attiyah and his cohorts. Why would the minister block me from leaving Doha yet again?

That night I didn't sleep. The next morning I was at the prosecutor's office at 7:00 a.m. I went to the front desk and asked for the public funds division. They took my ID card and told me to go to the seventh floor. I got there and most of the offices were closed. I found a police officer and told him I was looking for the public funds division. He told me that no one was there yet and ushered me to into a little room with benches. He told me to wait there.

In the room were two young men handcuffed together. I tried to ignore them.

I sat there for about two and half hours until finally the officer came to get me. He directed me to the office of the assistant prosecutor.

I knocked on his door and introduced myself. He knew who I was right away. I asked why there was a travel ban placed on me three hours after the court order ban had been lifted, and he told me that Wataniya and Qatar National Hotel had asked that the criminal complaint filed on February 7, 2010, by Wataniya, be reopened.

I asked what the public funds division of the prosecutor's office had to do with it. There was no public or government funds company. He said that the prosecutor general himself had asked them to review the file based on a request from Qatar National Hotels, a government-owned company and investor in Wataniya. I informed him that this matter was already settled and I had been cleared of any wrongdoing. He said that they were going to review the file and it shouldn't take long. I told him it sounded more like a witch-hunt.

I asked what accusations merited such an investigation. The assistant prosecutor was alleging that I had raised my own salary, received allowances I was not entitled to and mishandled company funds.

I informed the prosecutor that those accusations were old and baseless and that I had a court expert report and a judgment from a Qatari court that proved those allegations wrong. He requested I provide those documents, which I did that same day. The assistant prosecutor requested I come see him in one week.

So one week later, I went to see the assistant prosecutor, believing that after reviewing my documents I would be cleared and be able to leave Qatar. Instead, the assistant prosecutor asked me if I knew that Wataniya had filed a QR 50,000,000 civil lawsuit against me. I informed the assistant prosecutor that I was well aware of the civil case and that I had an attorney representing me in the matter. I was not worried about the civil case because it was frivolous, and 85% of the complaints had already been ruled in my favor with the final labor judgment. In addition, I had the necessary documents to support my position on the balance of the allegations. The assistant prosecutor asked me to submit those documents.

Within a few days, I complied with assistant prosecutor's request, and on February 15, I submitted all documents requested. I was told to come back in two weeks so they could have time to review the documents.

On February 22, 2011, I went to see the assistant prosecutor, and he informed me that he was waiting on documents and clarification from the company. He told me again to come back in two weeks.

So on March 3, 2011, I once again went to the see the assistant prosecutor. The company had added twelve new allegations, among them that I had falsified a payment to the landlord of the Egypt property for a penalty paid as a result of a fire, and also that I had hired a contractor for a major project and taken kickbacks.

He asked me if I had proof that these allegations were false. I told him I did, and he asked that I supply those documents. I refused and requested that the prosecutor show me the documents that the company had presented to substantiate their new claims. I also told him that it was not my responsibility to prove my innocence based on unsubstantiated allegations. The assistant prosecutor advised me to leave his office. He said he would notify me if they were going to file charges.

Feeling totally defeated, I went back home.

Chapter 10: Going Public

In late December 2010, I decided to put a little a pressure on Minister Khalid al-Attiyah, his family and the Qatari Government. Qatar is spending billions of dollars portraying itself as a modern, tolerant and cosmopolitan society. And at this precise time they were vying for the 2022 FIFA World Cup. Naturally, the royal family abhors any negative publicity or anything that sheds light on the reality that is Qatar.

Earlier that year, on January 29, 2010, Eric Ellis of *Euromoney Magazine* published an article entitled, "David Proctor: The Banker who couldn't get out of Qatar." The article caused a stir in Qatar, and he was released three months afterwards. I had met David in court shortly after the article came out. The bank had frozen his personal bank accounts. His situation was worse than mine, because he was a prominent British banker and former CEO of al-Khaliji Bank who had been kept in Qatar against his will for fourteen months. No charges were ever brought against David, who says his experience makes him caution others about doing business in Qatar. He was suddenly granted an exit visa to leave by the bank's chairman, Sheikh Hamad Bin Faisal Bin Thani al-Thani, shortly after the Ellis article came out. Prior to that, they just refused to release him or honor his contract. From what I understand, this is a typical tactic some Qataris employ as a way to get out of their financial obligations.

So in December 2010, with David's case in mind, I contacted my friend Tom Walsh, the business reporter for the *Detroit Free Press*. I had known

Tom for some time and had taken him and a delegation of other report-
ers and dignitaries with the former mayor of Detroit, Kwame Kilpatrick,
to Dubai in 2000. When I got through to Tom, he was shocked by my
situation and the fact that I had not gone public before. I told him that
I had thought antagonizing the Qataris early in the process would have
been counterproductive. But at that point, I was at my wit's end, and on
December 18, 2010, the *Detroit Free Press* ran a front-page article by Tom:
"Trapped in a foreign land."

That was the first shot over the al-Attiyahs' bow. They were comfortable in the view that they could do what they wanted to me without
any recourse, but I wanted to show them that I was not any ordinary
economic hostage. The article, I had heard through the grapevine, caused
some discomfort for Khalid, his brother and his cousin.

Now, after my second meeting with the assistant prosecutor, I decided to take my situation public. For over a year I had been silent. I had
felt that this was a personal matter and kept the details of my situation
confined to Maysa, my family and a few close friends. However, by now
I could see that this was going to get nasty. The al-Attiyahs were beginning to sense that they could not beat me in court and that I was not going to back down, and they were going to play dirty. I needed to escalate
this battle dramatically, into the public realm.

So with this new strategy in mind, the first thing I did was go back to
the embassy and inform them that my issue was no longer a legal one. I
had become an economic hostage; a Qatari minister and his family were
holding me.

On February 9, I sent the consular section the following email:

From: Nasser Beydoun
Sent: Wednesday, February 09, 2011 1:37 AM
To: Maha Dagistani
Subject: My Situation

Dear Maha,

*Please find attached a letter highlighting the harassment and persecution
I am currently facing. In the past, the embassy has taken a "hands off" approach because it was a legal matter. I have, for the grace of God, overcome and been victorious in all the legal hurdles placed in front of me over
the last 14 months. However, now the Minister and his partners have made
this a political issue by attempting to open a closed file at the prosecutor's*

office. What's more interesting is that this all happened only hours after I obtained my final travel restriction. Attached you will find all the details that highlight the situation and the supporting documents.

Respectfully yours,

Nasser M. Beydoun

I requested an immediate meeting with the ambassador, and I got an appointment with Ambassador Le Baron on March 20, 2011. Present in the meeting were Dao Le, the Senior Commercial Officer, and Alex Ave-Lallemant, Consular Section Chief.

I explained the new paradigms of my situation and tried to convince them that my situation was no longer legal but political in nature. The ambassador asked me some questions and asserted that he needed the proper information to approach the prosecutor general. He asked Alex to sit with me and prepare a one-page brief for this meeting. Approximately one week later, Ambassador Le Baron did indeed meet the Qatari Prosecutor General, Dr. al-Marri, and on March 28th I received the following email from Alex:

Nasser-

Hope you're doing well. I just wanted to let you know that the Ambassador managed to meet with the Attorney General before he left the country. He raised your case, pointing out that you just wanted to be able to visit your family and that you intended to return to Doha to continue legal proceedings. The Attorney General was aware of your situation. He told us that he was expecting an auditor's report on the case in "two or three weeks" and if the report came back clear you would be free to go.

Cheers,

Alex
Alex Ave-Lallemant
Consular Section Chief
U.S. Embassy
Doha, Qatar

This gave me a little hope that I might be out of Doha soon; however, his two to three weeks ended up being seven months. Unfortunately, it turned out that this was the most that Ambassador Le Baron would do. Again, one wonders whose interests the U.S. embassy—or in this case, the Ambassador personally, was there to serve and protect.

The Embassy did take a more active role when the Ambassador left that summer. After that, Alex was engaged, constantly in contact with the prosecutor general's office, putting pressure on them and keeping my situation high on the agenda.

That summer I read an article that appeared in the *Gulf Times* on July 20, 2011. In the article, Peter Townson writes:

> *U.S. Ambassador Joseph Le Baron bid farewell to members of the local and US business communities yesterday, where he described the "extraordinarily profound relationship" between America and Qatar as one of the most important in the world.*
>
> *Le Baron will leave government when he leaves Qatar on July 29, but he will be back later this year as he begins his life as a businessman in the country where he launched and ended his diplomatic career.*

To this day, I feel that if he had put the necessary pressure on the Qatari Government, my ordeal would have ended much sooner.

SETTING THE RECORD STRAIGHT

Over the past several months, Wataniya's leadership had been engaged in a concerted effort to destroy my reputation in Qatar. The effort was, I believe, a smokescreen. They needed a scapegoat because sales had dropped dramatically in the outlets that were still open. They had lost all of the brands to which I had secured the rights. They had destroyed the company, instead of injecting the 75 million riyals ($20.5 million) in new capital they had promised the shareholders at the General Assembly meeting on November 22, 2010.

I decided it was time to clarify all the misinformation that the al-Attiyahs had been telling people. I contacted a friend in Detroit, Leland Bassett. He and his wife, Tina, owned Bassett & Bassett, a PR company. Leland and Tina were shocked and did not hesitate to offer their services. I let him know that my financial situation would not allow me to pay him much. He told me, "Our main concern is to get you back to your family."

Then I contacted the man I considered my mentor, Ismael Ahmed. Ish, as he is known in Detroit, was the one of the pillars of the Arab-American community in United States. His work in civil rights and social services is legendary. Ish took me under his wing and guided my career, opened doors and helped me establish myself in the community. He had left ACCESS around the time I moved to Qatar and was appointed by then Michigan Governor Jennifer Granholm as the Director of Social Services for the State. He eventually settled as an Associate Provost at the University of Michigan-Dearborn.

I told Ish I needed his help, and he didn't flinch. He immediately went to work on securing me the assistance of Michigan's Democratic Congressional Delegation. I also contacted Ahmad Chebbani, Chairman of the American Arab Chamber of Commerce. Ahmad and I had worked together for years at the chamber, building it into one of the most powerful ethnic business organizations in the country. We also co-founded the U.S.-Arab Economic Forum. We had gone through the tragic events that unfolded after 9/11 and worked to protect the Arab American Business community from the aftermath.

I also contacted Chaker Aoun, a prominent local businessman. He and his wife Mona were among the few close friends who would constantly call Maysa and see if she needed anything. I had kept him and Ahmed updated on my situation. I also contacted Hassan Jaber, who had been Ish's deputy at ACCESS and took over as Executive Director when Ish left.

One of the first people to reach out to me and offer to assist was Talal (Lee) Turfe. Talal was an old family friend. His father, the late Hajj Ali Turfe, was one of the community's old timers. Hajj Ali's house was known as the White House of Dearborn.

Hajj Ali and my maternal grandfather were neighbors in Bint Jbail, Lebanon. When Hajj Ali's mom died when he was a child, my great grandmother would look after them. Talal was a retired executive from General Motors and a respected community leader. In the 70s and 80s Talal singlehandedly had helped employ hundreds of Lebanese immigrants at the Big Three auto companies. When he heard of my situation, he was appalled. He would later go on to say, "If I didn't help Nasser, my father would never forgive me."

He was very close to Michigan U.S. Senator Carl Levin and his brother, U.S. House Member Sander Levin. He was also a member of the Task Force on Lebanon, a Washington DC based organization that lobbied Congress for support for Lebanon. The Task Force members were the "who's who" of the Lebanese Diaspora in the United States. At one time I was a member. George Cody ran the Task Force with Deeb Keamy, his deputy.

Talal immediately contacted George and Deeb and they began to strategize on how best to help. George also contacted my friend in Houston, Nijad Fares, and briefed him. Nijad was an Executive Member and Vice Chairman of the American Task Force on Lebanon. He instructed George to do what was necessary to help me. Talal also got in touch with Senator Levin's office, while Ish, Ahmed and Hassan worked with Michigan U.S. Senator Debbie Stabenow and Michigan Congressman John Dingell.

I also reached out to my friend Harvey Bronstein. Harvey was a professor at Oakland Community College and was a respected member of Detroit's Jewish Community. Harvey and I had met in 2000 at a Seeds of Peace dinner. Harvey was a typical stereotype of a Jewish Liberal. He was one of the sweetest and most decent human beings I had ever met. He was an eternal optimist and one who worked to achieve peace in the Middle East. Harvey and his wife Marion became close friends of Maysa and me. The kids called him Uncle Harvey. Harvey and I had stayed in touch during my time in Qatar. He, too, had been in touch with Maysa and always inquired if she needed anything.

With my advocates in place, I began my publicity campaign.

FACEBOOK, TWITTER & THE MEDIA

We created a "Friends to Free Nasser" Facebook page and @freenasser Twitter account. In February of 2011, I issued my first post regarding my situation on Facebook. The response was heartfelt, and people were saying it was about time the facts came out. On March 1, 2011, I launched a website, www.qatarhostages.com. The website put all the information as it pertained to my situation in the public realm. It was a way to dispel the myths surrounding my situation and put the Qatari government on notice that I was not alone in this. From then on I started to post my progress using social media.

In the beginning of March, I received a call from Abdullah Berry. Abdullah was a friend and the son of Lebanon's Speaker of Parliament. It so happened that he was in Detroit at the time that my story broke and asked if he could help. Abdullah had grown up in Dearborn, and though we had never met, we had a lot of mutual acquaintances. He had returned to Lebanon and became active and powerful in his father's political party. He told me that he was going to contact Lebanon's Ambassador in Qatar, Hassan Saad. I had known Ambassador Saad for many years and met him when he was posted as the Counsel General to Lebanon in Detroit years prior. Our paths had crossed in Qatar on occasion. He was very active in the Diplomatic Corps in Qatar.

Abdullah told me to contact the ambassador. He said he would be able to assist me. I contacted him and he told me that he knew Khalid and Abdul Aziz al-Attiyah very well, and he would arrange a meeting to resolve our issues. He asked me how much I would be willing to pay them to settle this.

I was a little stunned. I told him that I was the one that had won the judgment and I wasn't willing to pay them anything. He said they were looking for retribution.

I told him they wouldn't get it from me and suggested that a meeting would not resolve anything. The only option to settle this matter was the courts. Since my travel ban was now from the prosecutor's office, I asked if he might be able to help with the prosecutor's office. He asked I write a letter to Dr. al-Marri and he would deliver it. So on March 7th, I sent him the following letter:

> *H.E. Dr. Ali bin Fetais al-Meri*
> *Prosecutor General*
> *Public Prosecution*
> *Doha*
> *State of Qatar*
>
> *Your Excellence,*
>
> *I am writing to respectfully request your assistance and highlight my plight and the injustices my family and I are currently enduring in Qatar. For the last fourteen months, I have been unable to work or to leave the country because of a frivolous 50 Million Riyal mismanagement civil lawsuit filed by my past employer, Wataniya Restaurant Company, in reprisal for a labor complaint I filed with the Qatari Labor Department and in full compliance with Qatari Labor Law. The main reason for my resignation was that I had not received a salary from that employer from May of 2009 until my last day of employment on November 23, 2009.*
>
> *On June 26th the Labor court awarded me QR 621,000 in my labor complaint, exonerating me of the frivolous charges filed by my past employer. On January 25, 2011, the judgment became final. On January 31, 2011, I was able to remove the travel ban imposed on me.*
>
> *However, even with that victory and vindication, I am still unable to travel, because that day a travel ban was imposed by the Public Prosecutors office. In meeting with the public funds section the following day, I was informed that a criminal complaint was reopened at the request of former employer. That complaint was originally closed by the prosecutor's office on February 8, 2010, for lack of merit. After one month of back and forth with the Prosecutor's office and presenting all documents requested, I was informed on March 3rd that the company has submitted two new charges. These charges are groundless and the company will use all means necessary to ensure I am delayed and impecunious in Qatar.*

Your Excellency, I moved to Qatar over three years ago, to take part in His Highness The Emir's vision and because of what Qatar had to offer: a modern society that provides all those who contribute to it certain human dignities and rights. However today, I find myself living a nightmare, unable to return home to my family who I have not seen in five months and having to request assistance from others to provide for my family.

I left the U.S. where I was a respected member of the community, the Chairman of the American Arab Chamber of Commerce, and moved to Qatar with my family. If you wish to ask about me, you need only ask H.E. Amre Moussa, Secretary General of the League of Arab States.

I have had my reputation attacked and smeared by board members and others, in their attempt to make me the scapegoat for all of the company's financial problems. I accept my responsibilities in full and can defend my actions; however the board refused to even meet with me and face me with their accusations. They only throw accusations of misconduct without a shred of evidence. In their lawsuit they attempt to manufacture evidence by submitting to the court partial submissions and misrepresentations, yet they have at their disposal the full documentation and facts. To string out the legal action they have resorted to, on more than one occasion, submitting their documents to the court in English, though the Qatari legal system requires all documents submitted to the court have to be in Arabic.

I tried to resolve this issue with Chairman, requested several meetings, only to be subject to abuse by his attorneys and a demand that I pay QR50 million "or else". I have no objection to defending myself against these ridiculous allegations in court. There is a civil case pending; let it proceed. Why do they fear it so? You are known to be a fair and honest man. I ask that your good office look at the merits of this case in an objective and impartial way. In advance thank you for your consideration of my request and your assistance in this matter.

Sincerely,

Nasser Beydoun

Ambassador Saad did indeed forward the letter to the Dr. al-Marri's office, and he told me to go see Adel Obaidly, his chief of staff. So shortly afterwards, I went down to the Prosecutor's and went to the 11th floor, which housed the prosecutor general's office and staff, as well as Adel's office. In my first meeting with Adel, he had told me that Ambassador Saad had informed him of my situation and he would do what he could to help. He asked me to submit a letter asking to lift the travel ban. I informed him that I had given the letter to Ambassador Saad, and he asked that I resubmit it to him. So the following day, I returned and gave him the previous letter. He told me to give him a couple of days and return.

The following week, I returned and he informed me that Dr. al-Marri had sent the letter to Saad Dossari for his comments and to come back in the following week.

When I returned at the prescribed date, he informed me that based on the information received from Saad Dossari, Dr. al-Marri denied my request. He asked me to submit another letter. So the following day, I submitted the same letter, just changed the date. Going back and forth several times, he again denied the request. This ping pong match would go on until my final release. But at the time, it was obvious that my release was not forthcoming.

My friends started to contact the Michigan Delegation to highlight my plight and get them engaged. On March 11, 2011, Senator Debbie Stabenow wrote a letter to the Qatari Ambassador to the U.S., Ambassador Ali Bin Fahad al-Hajri. It was followed on March 23 by a letter from Senator Carl Levin. On April 1, the Michigan Democratic Delegation chimed in with a letter cosigned by Congressmen John Dingell, John Conyers, Sander Levin, Gary Peters and Hanson Clarke with a letter to Ambassador al-Hajri. This added considerable political weight to my situation.

On March 18, my story went national when the Associated Press Detroit Correspondent Jeff Karoub wrote an article: "US Arab businessman says he's trapped in Qatar." On March 21, Nancy Kaffer of *Crain's Detroit Business* wrote an article: "Still trapped in Qatar: Can diplomacy free Beydoun?" I had worked with Nancy when she was a reporter at the *Dearborn Press & Guide* and the Chamber co-published a monthly magazine insert, "Community Bridges". I had known Keith Crain, the Editor in Chief, and Mary Kramer, the Publisher of *Crain's Detroit*. Over the years I had served on various civic committees with them. In fact, I was named to Crain's 40 under 40 in 2002 and Newsmaker of the Year in 2003, as well as being featured in *Crain's* several times.

To cap it off, on March 30, Curt Guyette of the *Detroit Metro Times* wrote an article: "Caught in Qatar." My situation was now viral on the web.

On March 27, 2011, having not heard from the prosecutor's office for over three weeks, I submitted a letter to the Qatari Prosecutor General Ali Bin Fetais al-Marri requesting that the travel ban be removed. I reiterated the facts that his office had already closed this case over one year prior and that I had a judgment in my favor that negated the vast majority of the allegations raised by my former employer and sponsor. I went on to say that this was a case of pure harassment and noted the ongoing civil matter in which a judge ruled to lift the travel ban, based on evidence submitted and accepted by the court.

I did not hear from his office, so I went several times to request an appointment to see him myself. I submitted, in all, four requests and went to his office over ten times during my interaction with the prosecutor's office, and he refused to meet with me. I kept wondering why Dr. al-Marri refused my many requests for a meeting. Everything I had heard about him was that he was incorruptible. He had a fine reputation and was known for his fairness. Yet he had placed a travel ban on me.

I tried to put myself in the same position. Whom would I have believed, a minister and respected member of Qatari society, or some foreigner? Khalid al-Attiyah had to protect his brother and cousin. Their lie had grown and kept growing.

I concluded that if I were to be allowed to leave Doha, that would reveal the al-Attiyahs' and Wataniya's claims of my embezzlement as false. It would deprive them of their scapegoat. In their attempt to shift the focus from Wataniya's new, incompetent general manager and management, they needed me in Qatar. And thus I had found myself with a new travel ban three hours after I removed the last one.

I believe the letters to the ambassador and to the U.S. Embassy in Qatar from the Michigan Delegation were very helpful. They got the State Department and the Embassy to focus on my situation. The letters to the ambassador served to put the government on notice. Dr. al-Marri could not have been anticipating this level of support. Now he had to act according to the rule of law, and not at the behest of Minister al-Attiyah and his family. The media, the letters, my friends in the Arab and Jewish communities and the social media push were exerting the necessary pressure. Even the Embassy started to get further engaged.

During the first three months of 2011, both the civil and labor lawsuits were ongoing.

On January 25th my labor judgment became final. Wataniya had no further recourse; they had to pay, or we would seize their assets and sell them in a public auction. I knew that Abdul Aziz and Hamid would never let that happen.

On February 27, we had a civil hearing to appoint a court financial expert to review the allegations and submit his finding to the court. To Mohsen's and my surprise, Wataniya recommended Khalid Askar. This was the same individual who did the report in the Labor lawsuit, and his report had been in my favor. We cautiously agreed, because we were apprehensive that they might have bought him off in the civil case. But these fears were unwarranted, and he proved to be a person of tremendous honor and respect for the law and the truth. However, with Wataniya's continued delays, it would take Khalid Askar over fourteen months to submit his findings.

In April 2011, I kept going back and forth to the prosecutor's office to keep the pressure on them. I submitted several requests to the prosecutor general to remove my travel ban, and they were all denied.

On April 14, Wataniya paid my judgment in full. I was pleasantly surprised that they did it. I had thought they would drag it out as much as possible. This concluded my labor case. I went with Adel to the court and collected the check, and then went immediately to the bank and deposited the check. I took out the cash I needed to pay legal fees and expenses and wired the balance to my account in the United States. I had learned from David Proctor not to leave any funds in the local bank. During the legal ordeal and my stay in Qatar, I kept all my money in cash. If I had Maysa transfer money to me, as soon as it cleared, I would withdraw it in cash. I would deposit a sum equal to my car payment one day before they withdrew it.

So with the judgment paid, in mid-April my family came to visit me. It was a wonderful re-energizing spring break. After they left, I put a renewed focus on the prosecutor's office.

THE AUDIT COMMITTEE

In late March I had learned that the prosecutor had appointed a three-person committee to audit the company, review their allegations, meet with me, and report their findings to the Public Funds division. The Prosecutor General had informed Ambassador Le Baron that the report would take several weeks. In reality, this committee had no time constraint by law and there was no legal recourse for me to pursue to force the committee to conclude their report. So I had to wait until the report was completed. They spent most of March and April at the Wataniya Corporate office, reviewing their files. Then towards the end of April, I received a call from one of the committee members and asked if I would meet with them at the prosecutor's office.

I agreed and asked if I needed to bring my attorney. They said only I could be present. So on May 3 at 9:00 a.m. I went down to the prosecutor's office. I went to the seventh floor, which is where the public funds division was located. I found the office for the committee. The committee was comprised of two Qataris and a Syrian gentleman, employees of the State Audit Bureau. The State Audit Bureau is an independent government body, directly reporting to H.H. the Emir. Its role is to scrutinize the accounts of all ministries and their affiliated departments and bodies, alongside with the accounts of public corporations, national companies and other government bodies. I went into the meeting and introduced myself. I told them I found it interesting that a government agency tasked to audit government entities was performing an audit for a private company on the behest of the public prosecutor.

Their reply was that they were completely independent and unbiased and would submit their findings solely on the facts. They proceeded to interview me for two days and over twelve hours.

A few days earlier, I had met with the assistant prosecutor, who had been given my case by the head of the Public Funds Department, who had previously threatened to put me in jail for ten years when I first met him. But after the facts started to come out, he became more supportive. And by the time he lifted the travel ban, he congratulated me and kissed me goodbye on the cheek.

As for the assistant prosecutor, from day one I sensed that he was not entirely convinced by the allegations against me. He didn't want to file charges in this case but was being pressured by the higher ups. Prior to my meeting with the audit committee, he went over the new accusations that Wataniya was alleging. This gave me time to put together my response in advance.

Unfortunately the accusations were more of the same thing: more embezzlement. I handed over all the judgments that were in my favor to prove my innocence.

As we went through the charges, the allegations after that became more petty and ridiculous. At one point during the meeting, I was so perturbed by the absurdity of these claims that I told the committee I was being held in the country for no reason, and that all they had provided me with were allegations without a shred of evidence. I also reminded them that I had most of the documents that proved my innocence.

I was informed that I didn't have to take part, but then the committee didn't know how long it would take to complete its report.

Wataniya had all this information on file as well, but they didn't provide it. They were hoping that I couldn't prove my innocence, so a criminal action would proceed against me and keep me in the country for several years. In addition, if criminal charges were filed, I would be imprisoned during the proceeding if I could not post a bond. This was their game plan. Word was that the al-Attiyahs' plan was to hold me for as long as they could, to set an example. Hamad al-Attiyah was throwing around the number of five years. Incredibly, I had most of the documents necessary to support my position.

On May 8th, we had a civil court hearing in which Khalid Askar, the court-appointed expert, was supposed to submit his report. However, Wataniya failed to provide any documents that substantiated their allegations, so the court scheduled the next hearing for June 27th.

During this period, I was working to get the documents I was missing. Elaine didn't have access to them. I tried the company auditors, because they would have signed off on them as part of their audit. They refused to provide the information.

After my initial meetings with the audit committee on May 3 and 4th, I went back to the prosecutor's office on a weekly basis to see if the audit committee had reached any conclusions.

On May 23rd, Wataniya finally submitted their supporting documents to the court expert who, in theory, was supposed to substantiate their allegations. However, what they submitted was over 32 binders of documents with new allegations of impropriety against me totaling 230 million riyals ($63 million). Each document had over one thousand pages, and 98 percent of them were in English. Their objective was simple: to ensure that the court expert could not meet his deadline and submit his report at the June 27th Civil hearing. They succeeded in ensuring that the civil case would be postponed until after the court's summer recess.

Mohsen, my attorney, called me and told me that the court expert had delivered the boxes to his office and they took up his entire conference room. He asked if I would come and go through them and review the new allegations.

I went that same day. I started going through each binder, and to my surprise, what Khalid al-Attiyah's attorneys had done was basically to submit every document that had anything to do with my tenure at the company. I don't think they knew or cared what they submitted. They just made copies, boxed everything, and sent it to the expert. They wanted to buy time. In reality, this was a God-send, as what they did was give me the remaining documents I needed to prove my innocence with the audit committee.

I showed the information to Mohsen, and he was as pleasantly surprised as I was. So, the question was whether we should provide this information to the prosecutor general or wait to see what the committee did. If he proceeded with criminal charges, we would have the proof that I was innocent. Basically, should we tip our hand?

Mohsen and I pondered that question; it boiled down to a basic matter of time. If I provided the audit committee with the missing information to prove my innocence, then the report would be submitted finding me innocent of the allegations. But how independent was this committee, and would the report be used to prove my innocence or find or create the scenario where criminal charges would be filed?

I finally decided that since I had all the documents I needed to prove my innocence, I had nothing to lose. If I left everything up to the committee, they controlled how long it would take. My main objective was to remove the ban the prosecutor had placed on me. The civil case was no longer stopping me from leaving because I had a guarantor (or what you could call a surrogate hostage). I decided to try and force the prosecutor's hand.

On June 1, I went to see the assistant prosecutor. I told him that I had the balance of the documents to prove that I was innocent of all the accusations leveled by the company. I proposed submitting them to the committee, and asked if the company would be able to continue to add charges to waste time. He told me not to worry about that, and advised me to provide the committee the information so their report would come back in my favor and the prosecutor general would have to release me.

On the day I went to the audit committee's office to present the documents and go through them with the committee, I again asked if I had shown without a doubt that all the company's claims against me were fabricated and that the two most serious charges were sheer fabrications.

They agreed, and said that when this was done, I would have the right to seek retribution. This provided little solace, however, because I still did not have any indication what their report would find.

They took the documents, added them as exhibits, and amended my statement to reflect the submissions. Then they told me that they needed to print my statement and have me read it for accuracy and sign it.

I don't read Arabic, so I asked if he could read the report to me. He said he could bring someone to read it for me. I immediately called my attorney Mohsen, explained the situation and asked if he would come down. I waited until he arrived.

When he arrived, the committee asked his relationship to me. I informed him that he was my attorney. They informed us that he could not act in his capacity as my legal counsel, render any legal advice or make any changes to my statement. He could only read the report out loud. I found it odd that I could not have legal representation, but we agreed. I figured at least he would have an idea of what was in my statement, and I could trust him. They would not even provide me a copy of the statement, which was worrisome.

Now the committee had everything they needed from me, and it was only a waiting game for the report to come out. I continued to go on a weekly basis to the prosecutor's office to see if the report had been submitted.

On June 6th, Mohsen set up a meeting for us to respond to the new allegations with the same individual who had filed the labor report, Khalid Askar. He was perplexed and very hostile at the beginning of the meeting, and I sensed in his tone that he was tilting towards them. He was also weary of all the documents that Wataniya had submitted. He said that he was going to ask the court to increase his fee because of the sheer volume of work involved in the report.

Mohsen reiterated that this just a stalling tactic and that if they were serious, they would have translated the documents into Arabic in accordance with the law. I briefly explained our position and that the very documents they presented would exonerate me. He asked Mohsen to prepare a response to the allegations.

On June 27th we had another civil court hearing, where again Khalid did not submit his report, and the court scheduled a subsequent hearing on September 12th after the summer break.

On July 6th, on one of my many visits to the prosecutor's office, I was told that my visits would not expedite the report, and because of the seriousness of the charges, I should let it take its course.

With summer and Ramadan approaching it was becoming obvious that I would not get out of Doha before the Islamic Eid holiday. However, I kept the pressure on the committee, calling regularly to get them to submit their report, until the day I received a phone call from someone in the prosecutor's office who firmly advised to stop calling the committee or I would be charged with obstructing the investigation.

How ironic. I was trying to expedite it because I was the only one suffering from the situation. All the al-Attiyahs could travel and had no fallout. I was the only one who was stuck in Qatar, without a job and without my family. So I adjusted my expectations and recognized that I would have to spend another summer stuck in Qatar.

CHAPTER 11: THE REAL DOHA, BEHIND THE FANCY FAÇADE

The longer I stayed in Doha, the more I understood that how Qatar portrays itself to the outside world is nothing but a façade. Doha is like a Hollywood movie set. It looks impressive from a two-dimensional aspect but has no depth. Behind the curtain there is a void.

During my time in Doha, it was a city in upheaval, in transition, and on the move, with no map to follow. Entire sections were being torn down and new sections were coming up, but nothing seemed to make sense or get done on time. Major infrastructure projects, such as the New Doha International Airport, were years behind scheduled completion. Road projects would start and seem to never finish. If they were completed, they were constantly dug up again.

The new Hamad Medical Center that housed the athletes for the 2006 Asia Games sits as an empty shell. The Islamic Museum was completed; it was an impressive I. M. Pei design, yet the exhibits inside left a lot to be desired. It seemed that Qatar was trying to create a cultural identity that never existed. It was a *nouveau riche* mentality: they were trying to buy culture and education and create class and prestige. Even the souvenirs, if you could find any, were fake. The newly built "Old Souk" sells flimsy little "antique camel-bone" boxes, some of them still bearing little gold labels, "Made in India."

During the majority of my time in Doha, I lived in the Dafna section which, as I mentioned earlier, was land reclaimed from the sea. Dafna is considered the new downtown of Doha, because of the impressive amount of high-rise buildings under construction. Prior to Qatar's economic boom, Dafna was considered the outskirts of Doha, where the main post office, the Sheraton Hotel and several government ministers, courts, prosecutor's office and Qatar Petroleum were located. In the past ten years, new high-rise buildings began to spring up around the newly built City Center Mall. In 2007, the new Four Seasons Hotel and Apartments opened, owned by the Prime Minister Sheikh Hamad bin Jassim al-Thani. As Qatar boomed, hotels, commercial and residential towers sprung up. So did taxis, briefly. (Then the royal family created a monopoly of the taxi business, gave themselves ownership of it, and reduced the number of cars available. Drivers—Bangladeshis, Somalis and others—queue up for an hour in the morning and pay for the privilege of leasing a car for the day, in hopes of making more than they invested.)

From my apartment, I watched the boom and bust that was the reality of Doha. Doha in 2006 and 2007, as stated, was booming. However, the financial crisis of 2008 put the brakes on Qatar's dreams of being the next Dubai. Where Dubai had industry, population, tourism, shopping, hotels, prostitution, a world-class airport and a thirty-year head start, Doha had only a government whose coffers were beginning to overflow with gas dollars. The Qatari government was either in denial or wanted to paint the opposite picture, and Doha was affected.

The many announcements that Qatar was building the world's tallest, the biggest and the most luxurious masked the fact that only a fraction of those ambitious projects ever saw the light of day. Fewer still reached completion. The private sector was on life support. Qatari government and infrastructure projects were still ongoing, though they seemed to slow down. Qatari Government investment in the gas and downstream sectors continued. This sector solely accounts for the increase in GDP and the country's economic growth figures.

The Qatar Foundation also kept up an impressive construction schedule. The government could afford to keep its projects going because of the surplus of gas dollars, estimated at $100 million per day. This is a very impressive figure for a native population of 250,000.

Today Dafna offers an impressive picture and is often used to promote Doha as a modern cosmopolitan city. In reality, most of the high-rise buildings are completed on the outside and unfinished on the inside. There are no official vacancy rates, but while government ministers occupy a portion of various buildings, the rest sit vacant. Many of the signature projects, such as the 90-story QNB Tower, 110-story Doha Tower and the 90-story Jerusalem Tower, never got off the ground.

At one time, the ruler of Dubai, Sheikh Mohamed bin Rashid al-Maktoum, was going to build a 90-story mixed used tower at the foot of the cornice heading into Dafna. The story goes, since the Emir of Qatar presented the land to Sheikh Mohamed, Sheikh Mohamed was going to present the building as a gift to the Emir. Because of Dubai's financial meltdown, to this day the Dubai tower stands idle as a 30-story skeleton, and there is no start or completion date on the horizon. Only two of the five hotels surrounding the City Center were completed after years of little movement. With Qatar hosting the 2022 FIFA World Cup, Doha needs to add over 60,000 hotel rooms, which seems an impossible task, given Qatar's history of failing to meet deadlines or complete projects. I used to wonder, even if they did add all those rooms, what would they do with them when the event is over?

LIFE ON THE PEARL

To get to the Pearl from Doha, you take the Lusail road. Lusail is the newest planned city in Qatar, being developed by the state-controlled developer Qatari Diar Real Estate Investment Company. It's located on the coast about 15 km (9.32 Miles) north of the city center of Doha, just north of the West Bay Lagoon. The master plan envisions a city of up to 250,000 people situated on 35 km² (21.75 sq. mi.). Lusail will house marinas, residential areas, island resorts, commercial districts, luxury shopping and leisure facilities, including two golf courses (how much irrigation does that imply?) and an entertainment district.

Driving to the Pearl, you will pass Doha's new Diplomatic Quarter that houses a number of foreign embassies. On the coast are some of the vast palaces owned by Qatar's rulers. The Intercontinental Hotel and the newly constructed St. Regis Complex, as well as a cultural eyesore called Katara Cultural Village, are on your right, before you reach the West Bay Lagoon. The Katara website states that: "Katara was born out of a long held vision to position the State of Qatar as a cultural beacon, a lighthouse of art, radiating in the Middle East through theatre, literature, music, visual art, conventions and exhibitions." You turn right when you reach the ZigZag towers to see two of the ugliest buildings you will ever lay your eyes on. Then you pass the newly completed Grand Hyatt, and in the distance, the Ritz Carlton Doha on your left. As you enter the Pearl, you are impressed by the bridge the takes you on the island, as well as the manicured landscaping and flowing water features.

When I moved to the Pearl in October 2010, I started in a small two-bedroom apartment but I would move four times before finally being released. This was my sanctuary as well as my prison. The Pearl-Qatar, as it was known, is a master planned development built by United Development Company (UDC), a Qatari Company, one of Qatar's largest listed private companies on the Qatar Stock Exchange.

This was supposed to be Qatar's Riviera, a man-made island, reclaimed from the bay. This island-building trend in the Gulf was started by Dubai's Palm Island. And true to form, what Dubai did, Abu Dhabi, Bahrain and Qatar were sure to follow.

This offshore, 400 hectares (985 acres) manmade island comprises two bays, ten sectors, 60 residential towers, residential villages, over 410 villas, 3 luxury hotels, 3 marinas, and other facilities for retail, entertainment, dining, and education. I lived in Porto Arabia, a bay surrounded by 31 Mediterranean-style towers with a total of 4,700 units, 450 townhouses and low-rise terrace apartments, 1,000,000 square feet of leasable retail and commercial spaces and 2.5 kilometer (1.55mile) 'La Croisette Boulevard' cornice. The bay is the future home of the new Four Seasons hotel (also owned by the Prime Minister Hamad bin Jassim al-Thani) on a central islet and a 785-berth marina.

When I left Qatar in October 2011, only 11 of the towers were completed. The remainder was stalled with very little activity. The three promised hotels were only pilings. The retail podiums and townhouses were complete, yet a majority sat empty. There was an area that mirrored the canals of Venice. And at the tail of the island was a cluster of manmade islands with stunning bay views, which were to house palaces for Qatar's royal family. Ironically, one of those miniature islands was gifted by the emir to Syrian President Bashar al-Assad, when they were on better terms.

The Pearl was the brainchild of Hussain Ebrahim Alfardan, and he serves as the Chairman of the Board of United Development Corporation, the master developer of The Pearl. Alfardan is a Qatari citizen of Persian origin, a Shi'a Muslim, and his family were prominent pearl merchants in the Arab gulf prior to the oil boom and the invention of synthetic pearls. To this day, he has one of the largest private collections of natural Gulf pearls in the world and is regarded as one of the world's experts in natural pearls. He started his career at the age of 21, when he established his first business, Alfardan Jewelry Est. For the last fifty years, he has managed the Alfardan Group Holding Co., which has the sole distribution rights for some of the world's most luxury brands in Qatar. Alfardan

Group is known in Qatar for trading of jewelry, watches, automobiles, as well as money exchange. Their group includes Rolls Royce, Ferrari, Maserati cars; Piaget, Patek Philippe Watches. They have vast investments in real estate, including luxury projects such as Alfardan Gardens gated communities, St. Regis Hotel and the seventy story Kempinski Apartment Suites in Dafna (Qatar's tallest building). Mr. Alfardan was the driving force for Qatar's first private bank, The Commercial Bank of Qatar (CBQ) and since inception serves as the managing director.

It's worth noting that CBQ was Wataniya's bank and the current chairman is Abdullah Bin Khalifa al-Attiyah. Both Alfardan and al-Attiyah started their careers in the procurement office of the Qatari Army.

The retail section of the island was envisioned to house so many of the world's most luxurious brands that it would have made Rodeo Drive look like a middle class shopping venue. Alfardan opened his Rolls Royce, Ferrari and Maserati showrooms. Alfardan Jewelry prominently displayed some of the finest watchmakers and jewels in their jewelry outlet. Hermes, Canali, Salvatore Ferragamo, Massoni, Armani, Stefanio Ricci, Roberto Cavelli, Calvin Klein as well as other boutiques peppered a section of the retail podium. Alfardan brought in some of the world's best restaurants, such as Gordan Ramsay's Maze, Bice Ristorante, from New York Magoo and The Chocolate Bar, Richard Sandoval's Pompano as well as other bistros and coffee shops.

One of the redeeming qualities of life on the Pearl was that the only time you needed to leave was to go grocery shopping. None of the promised grocery stores had opened during my time there. Nonetheless, I noticed that more and more people started moving there because the rents were equivalent to lesser areas of Doha, and most of the restaurants, until they were banned from doing so in March 2011, served alcohol. This made it an attractive location for expatriates. Prior to the Pearl, only five-star hotels were allowed to serve alcohol.

There is only one store in Qatar to buy alcohol; it's owned by Qatar Airways. The rumor mill in Doha was that the revenue from liquor sales subsidized the airline. You need a permit to buy alcohol, and in order to get a permit, you need to have a certain classification of residence permit and the approval of your Qatari sponsor. In addition, you are given a monthly limit to spend on alcohol. During the month of Ramadan, the liquor store would close, but the government would double the limit for the preceding month. The day before Ramadan, the liquor store was like Black Friday, the day after Thanksgiving in the U.S., the biggest shopping day of the year: it was a madhouse with expatriates stocking up on alcohol.

The irrational liquor policy extended to the restaurants on the Pearl. For instance, Pompano, the Mexican restaurant could serve Tequila, but not vodka or whiskey. Burj al Hamam, which served Lebanese cuisine, could serve Arak (Lebanese Ouzo) but not any other hard liquor. Magoo, the Japanese Sushi restaurant, could only serve Sake, wine and beer, and the Italian restaurants were regulated to beer and wine. When the government revoked the liquor sales, several of the restaurants closed their doors, causing millions of dollars in investment losses. This wasn't the first time that government policy, either lack of or reversal of, on the Pearl caused businesses and expatriates to suffer.

The selling point of the Pearl was that expatriates who bought units would be granted residence in Qatar. Many foreigners bought real estate due this fact alone, including some of my friends. Yet when they went to take possession of their property, the developer UDC reneged on the residence promise because the government had not approved the residence law or provided a mechanism for implementing it.

Thus, you could own a unit and if your work visa was revoked, you could be deported. Worse yet, if you had a bank loan and were in default, the bank could impose a travel ban. Another issue many of the buyers faced is when they went to take possession of their units, some of the developers hit them with exorbitant utility connection fees, though there was never any mention of these fees prior. The developer's excuse was that these were fees passed on from UDC. If tenants refused to pay, the developer refused to hand over to them their units.

Day to Day Life

"In prison, those things withheld from and denied to the prisoner become precisely what he wants most of all." — *Eldridge Cleaver*

The Pearl was my prison. The only thing withheld from me was my ability to leave Qatar and be reunited with my family. I spent each day hoping that this would be my last day in Qatar. I vowed to never let the al-Attiyahs destroy me. I didn't know when or if there would come a day when I would be thrown in a Qatari jail. I created a routine that kept my spirits high. I would wake in the morning and work out. Then I would drink a double espresso and spend some time reading several U.S. newspapers. I would usually read the *Detroit Free Press* and *Detroit News*, the *New York Times*, and the *Washington Post*. Then I would read the *Gulf*

Times to see what was happing in Qatar or read the *Naharnet* to see what was going on in Lebanon, followed by the Israeli *Haaretz*. I would check out Google News to catch some interesting articles. I would then see what family and friends were up to on Facebook and add some posts on my Facebook page and Twitter.

After that I would have a bite to eat and do some more reading. eBooks gave me access to the outside world, and Google allowed free access to many of the great works of literature that were out of copyright. I read or reread all the classics, mostly biographies of great world leaders.

Maysa, back home, was working fulltime and taking care of the kids. She made sure that their lives were as normal as possible. Every day after lunch, I would call them on Skype, before they went off to work and school. Then I would start making calls to family and friends.

In the evening I would go for a walk on the island. I would time my walk and go around the full length of the boardwalk, about a mile and half, and sit at the end and watch the sunset. It was a time to reflect and meditate and gather my thoughts and strength for the next day. In the evening I would stop at one of the coffee shops for a cigar.

I sold my car in April, and after that I rarely ventured off the island. I would go into Doha to see my attorney or to grocery shop. Once in awhile, my friend would come by and pick me up and we would have dinner and a shisha at the Old Souk or go to another friend's place for dinner off the island.

I tried to maintain a low profile, not knowing if they might try and entrap me or create an incident that might jeopardize my freedom. Late in the evening, I would watch a movie to pass the time away. I had signed up for Netflix, but unfortunately it didn't work overseas, so I set up a remote VPN that gave me a U.S. IP, allowing me to circumvent the Qatari security services and access Netflix: such controversial material as old episodes of Monk, Rockford Files or Hawaii Five-O, which brought back memories of my childhood in Dearborn and a much simpler time.

I also copied and scanned all my documents and put them in remote files online. I left copies with friends, and Maysa had access via the Internet.

THE FINAL DAYS

In April my landlord sold the apartment and moved me to another one. He allowed me to renew my lease for a three-month period at a time. As August approached, my lease was up and he wanted to raise my rent.

I couldn't afford the new rent, so I started looking for another accommodation. A friend told me that her neighbors were going back to Europe for a month and wanted someone to house-sit their cats. That took me through to September 1.

In 2011, Ramadan, the Muslim holy month, fell in August. Most schools would not reopen until after the Eid Holiday in September, so most of the expatriate families would not return. The country was a ghost town. As Ramadan 2011 was approaching, I consoled myself that nothing was going to happen during this time.

To make things a little brighter, Maysa and I had decided that they would come spend Ramadan with me, and they arrived August 1st.

During Ramadan, most shops were operating on Ramadan hours: they would open for a few hours in the morning, then close. They would reopen in the evening after the feast was over. Restaurants other than those in hotels would close all day and open only in the evening. The only thing open was the supermarkets and the movie cinemas, so we spent most of the day at home or at the pool. Doing nothing made it the best month. We didn't do anything but be together. I savored every minute with them, and my problems seemed to be a distant memory. But as Labor Day approached, they had to go back to Michigan.

Now the owners of the apartment I was living were coming back, and I had to find a new place to live again. I thought I was going to have to move in with a friend who had a small one-bedroom apartment in Dafna, but another friend in my apartment complex left for Cleveland for the Eid holiday, and he gave me his I apartment for a couple of weeks.

On September 6th I went to the prosecutor's office to check on the status of the audit committee report. The prosecutor was still on vacation, so I went to see his supervisor, Ahmad Abdul Wahab. I walked into Ahmad's office and kissed him and wished him a Happy Eid. This was a customary greeting. By then, he and I had transformed our relationship from one of prosecutor–defendant to a respectful one. He smiled at me and informed me that the committee had submitted their report, but he had not reviewed it. But he said the prosecutor would be back the next day, so I should come back then.

This was some kind of progress. At that stage, I didn't care what the report said; I was just glad that it was done. So on the 8th I went to see the prosecutor. He saw me coming and smiled. He said, "I know why you are here, but I just got back and haven't read the report." He needed a week to review it.

Well, I thought, I've waited all this time. A week wasn't going to kill me.

On the 15th I went back. He informed me that the report had found no criminal activity on my part and that he had forwarded it to Dr. al-Marri to sign off on. He asked if I wanted to read it. I said that I didn't read Arabic, and I was content that it found me innocent of any wrongdoing.

I was ecstatic and glad that I was finally vindicated. I immediately called Maysa, then my father.

Ultimately, I would end up going back to the prosecutor's office five times, because Dr. al-Marri was in and out of town and had not signed off on the report. On Thursday, October 6th I went to the prosecutor's office around 9:00 a.m. Usually I would go around 11:00 a.m.

I got to the 7th floor and no one was there, so I went to the 11th floor, where Dr. al-Marri's office was. As I got off the elevator, I saw everyone who worked in the prosecutor's office. They saw me coming and greeted me with a big smile and warm hello, and then they congratulated me and told me Dr. al-Marri had just signed off on my release.

I was ecstatic; I kissed them all and thanked them for allowing the truth to come out. Even though it took nine months and over one hundred visits to the prosecutor's office, I was happy this ordeal was done.

Sultan, one of the prosecutors, congratulated me on my demeanor throughout the ordeal. He said that as difficult as my situation was, I was always a perfect gentleman in my dealings with them. He wished me luck.

Then Saad, another one, walked me down to his office and invited me in. This was the first time he had allowed me in his office. He asked his secretary to type up my release, and within five minutes, the secretary returned with a letter. Saad signed it and faxed it to the Interior Ministry to remove my travel ban. I had to now wait to get an SMS message from the ministry that the travel ban was lifted.

However, I called a friend and asked him to pick me up. I wanted to confirm that no other travel restrictions were in place. So we headed to the Main Police Station in Downtown Doha. I went to the investigations division and requested to see the officer in charge. I explained my situation and asked him to check if I had anything other than the prosecutor's travel ban in my file. He looked and informed me that there was another travel ban in place by the al-Rayyan Police Station.

Al-Rayyan is a community on the outskirts of Doha. It was seat of power of the Emir before the current Emir's father overthrew him and took over. It is also where Khalid and Abdul Aziz bin Mohamed's father was particularly well known and powerful. This was their area, and I began to wonder if they had placed that ban using their political power.

The officer told us to go to Rayyan and see what the situation was. Ameen and I headed there immediately. It was about a twenty-five minute car ride. When I got there, I knew where to go because this was the same spot that I had gone to for the first travel ban. I asked the officer why they had a travel ban on me, when the prosecutor had lifted his ban.

The officer went upstairs for about twenty minutes and came down and told me that since the prosecutor had lifted the ban, they would take off their ban. I asked what the purpose of their ban was, but he could not give me an answer. I asked how long would it take, and he said that they were entering it now.

By that point it was Thursday afternoon, and government offices were starting to close down. My friend and I decided to double check, so we went back to the main police station. We went to the same officer and requested he check again. He said that both travel bans were still in place. Then I remembered that there was a general who was related to Abdullah al-Jufairi, the vice chairman of Wataniya from Detroit who worked in the investigations division in the same complex. We walked over to where he worked, and they told me that he had just left. It was late and the government offices had closed. If the bans were lifted, I would receive a message on my phone.

I went back home, which by now was another apartment on the Pearl, with Neil McCauley, who was the group head of special assets at CBQ. Neil was initially in charge of trying to recover the Wataniya loan that had gone bad. I had met him about a year earlier when Fares Mootasem, my loan officer at the bank, had introduced me to him. Our first meeting was a lunch meeting at the bank with the three of us. He had heard all the false accusations and lies about me—Wataniya had made it sound as if I had ripped off the company for tens of millions of dollars. At lunch that day, Neil went over all the accusations. I was prepared and presented all the documents that invalidated all their claims and noted that every dollar spent from the bank funds was supported by the proper draw requests. I also informed him that if any items submitted were not valid or fraudulent, the al-Attiyahs would not have hesitated to throw me in jail.

At lunch that day, I presented a plan for the bank to seize the company. We would salvage the assets and turn the company around. Neil liked the plan; more importantly, he was a man of integrity, and at the end of the meeting, he understood that I was being railroaded. He went back to his superiors with his recommendations and a solid plan to recover the loan. However, his superiors were not about to upset the al-Attiyahs. They dismissed the idea and failed to act, and the company continued to deteriorate.

During the remainder of my time in Qatar, Neil and I became good friends. We would have breakfast together almost every Friday, and on occasion, dinner. So when I had to find another new apartment, Neil invited me to live with him. We kept the arrangement a secret. He had nothing to gain from helping me, but he knew it was the right thing to do. I really appreciate the risk he took in letting me stay with him.

When I got back "home" that day, Neil was in London, so I gathered my belongings and waited for the SMS. I had very little clothing left in Doha, since I had been sending things home every time someone went back to Michigan. In fact, all I had left in Doha fit in one suitcase. My bags were packed and I was ready to go. But that evening nothing happened.

I spent Friday and Saturday waiting.

On Sunday morning, I went down to the prosecutor's office to see Saad and let him know that the travel ban was still in place and that there was another ban in place by the al-Rayyan police department. He seemed astonished by the news. He asked his secretary to resend the removal to the Department of Interior. Then he proceeded to give me a letter to take to the al-Rayyan station, instructing them to remove the ban. He told me to go to them, and if they had any issues, to have the officer call him.

I immediately headed to al-Rayyan and went again to see the officer in charge and gave him the letter. He told me that the ban would be removed. I called Ahmed, my sponsor, and we went to his office to get the exit permit.

On the way, I received an SMS from the Minister of Interior that my travel ban was lifted. I didn't know which one it was, but that was great. After I got to Ahmed's office, we all got in the car and proceeded to the passport office by the Qatar Foundation. Ahmed had a friend who worked there.

Ahmed submitted the paper work for my exit permit. The gentleman at the counter checked the computer and told us that there was still a travel ban. We went back to the al-Rayyan police station. Once again, we were told it was removed.

Back to the main police station again. I went to see General Mohammad al-Jufairi, Abdullah's cousin. Over the weekend, I had called Sam Sheikh and asked him to call Abdullah's other cousin, Abdul Rahman al-Jufairi. Abdul Rahman was a respected lawyer in Doha and a shareholder in Wataniya. He was intimately aware of my situation and had tried to help me early on. But once he had determined that the al-Attiyahs were not susceptible to an amicable resolution, he distanced himself. However, I would meet with him on occasion and he would review my situation and give me his opinion. I appreciated the moral support he provided and the encouragement. Sam asked Abdul Rahman to call his cousin, General Mohamed, and persuade him to assist.

During these few days we had kept my situation very confidential. I did not let anyone know that the prosecutor had lifted the ban, for fear that it might get back to the al-Attiyahs and they would try and stop me somehow. Hardly anyone in Doha knew.

True to his word, Abdul Rahman called the general, and he greeted us warmly when we got there. He checked his computer and told me the prosecutor's ban had been lifted but the al-Rayyan ban was still in place. He was baffled as to how al-Rayyan could have a ban in place when the prosecutor's office had lifted theirs. He advised us to go back to al-Rayyan and see why it wasn't removed.

Once again, we headed to the al-Rayyan police station. I informed the officer that the ban was still not lifted and that I would go in the morning to the prosecutor's office and file a formal complaint if they did not lift the ban. The officer told me that his superior had gone for the day and that he would call him and get to the bottom of it. He instructed us to return in the morning.

The next morning, on Monday, October 10th, Ameen and I got there around 7:30 a.m. I went to the front desk; I think they knew I was coming. The minute I asked to see the officer in charge, they informed me there was no need. The travel ban had been lifted.

I called Ahmed and informed him, but I told him I was going to see General al-Jufairi at the main police station to confirm. Ameen and I headed to the central Doha station. When we arrived at the police station, we proceed to General al-Jufairi's office.

I asked him to check to see if the ban was lifted. He checked his computer and said that I was cleared to leave. I was cautiously euphoric, but would not allow myself to be fully satisfied until I left Doha. Too many unexpected things had gone wrong until this point.

I immediately called Ahmed to meet me at the passport office at the airport. He told me he needed about an hour, so Ameen and I went back home and picked up my bag.

When we arrived, sure enough, Ahmed was waiting for us. We waited in line, and when our turn came, the young lady checked the computer and told us that I was clear to leave, but that this office no longer issued exit permits. We would have to go to the Wakra office.

Wakra was about ten minutes from the airport. All three of us immediately ran to the car and proceeded to the Wakra office. We got there, and in about fifteen minutes obtained my exit permit.

Still not believing that I would be leaving, we went to the airport. I was going to get on the first flight out of Doha, regardless of where it was going. It was about 10:00 a.m. There was a flight to Dubai at 11:30 a.m., or one to Beirut at 2:00 p.m. I knew that Aboudi was traveling to Beirut, so I bought a ticket to Beirut.

I checked in and proceeded to head through customs. I was almost out, but still thinking that at any moment I would be denied leaving. I went to the Qatar Airways lounge; Aboudi met me there and we waited for the flight. We sat there for about three hours, praying that this nightmare was finally over. As Aboudi and I were sitting in the lounge, who did we see but Donald Jordan, the person who had recruited me for Wataniya. I approached Donald and said hello. He was surprised to see me. I asked him not to contact anyone and let them know that I was at the airport, leaving.

Finally they called our flight and Aboudi and I boarded the plane. As soon as the plane took off, my friends Ameen and Bilal lit up the social networks with pictures and news of my departure. Maysa and the kids had left Qatar on October 10th 2010, and I left on October 10th, 2011, exactly one year to the day.

Arriving in Beirut

We arrived in Beirut at about 6:00 p.m., and I felt a freedom I hadn't known in over a year. I cannot explain the feeling. At the airport, my relatives and friends embraced me. We went to my Aunt Zienab's for dinner. It is customary; every time I flew to Beirut, the first stop would be Aunt Zienab. She would always have a southern Lebanese delicacy prepared: frakeeh, raw beef mixed with spices and cracked wheat.

The next day, Aboudi and I went to Bint Jbail to see my dad. We finished closing up the house for the winter, saw my cousin Jamal and paid a visit to the cemetery where my grandparents and my uncles Mahmoud and Mohammad were buried. We spent the night in Bint Jbail.

The next morning, we packed up my dad and went to the next village, Barchit, to see my Aunt Naziha and her husband, Abu Hasim. My aunt had just completed rebuilding her house that was destroyed in the 2006 war with Israel. She told me a story that my grandfather would say: a true measure of a man is if he falls onto hard times and emerges stronger than before.

The next morning, my dad and I flew back to Detroit.

Detroit

The flight to Detroit seemed endless. I couldn't help thinking when I land in Detroit, I would have to rebuild my life. I would have to get reacquainted with my wife, my children. Get used to having my family around me again. I had lost most of my investments in Michigan because of my inability to travel back and forth. My reputation was tattered and I didn't know what to expect from all my friends and former associates. But that took a backseat to the excitement of coming home. We landed in Detroit around 4:00 p.m.

All the media attention that I had received during my captivity had brought me a tremendous amount of publicity. As soon as we arrived at customs, two agents approached me and welcomed me home. They advised me that there was great deal of media waiting for me; Leland Basset had been busy bringing my plight to the public's attention so no one else would ever have to go through what I had.

My dad and I claimed our bags, cleared customs and walked through the security area to my waiting family. The first to greet me was my daughter Jana. She had a bouquet of flowers. Then my son Jamal came running and jumped into my arms. A front-page picture captured that moment the following day in the *Detroit Free Press*. Then Aya and Maysa greeted me.

My mom was so excited to see me, she forgot my father was with me. My sisters and brother, nieces and nephews were all there. After that, I did several media interviews and we all returned to my parent's house for a large family dinner. After seven hundred and ninety one days since my last visit to the United States, it was great to finally be home.

CHAPTER 12: MOVING ON

In the end, it took me six hundred and eighty six days; over two hundred thousand dollars in expenses; fourteen court hearings in my labor case; thirteen court hearings (and still counting) in the frivolous civil lawsuit that Wataniya filed against me; five visits to the Human Rights department and forty-one interactions with the Qatari Prosecutor's office to win my freedom and rescind my travel ban.

The numbers, when boiled down like that, are shocking, but the true horror came from the fact that I was denied access to my family for no reason. I cannot put a value on every day spent away from them, away from my children growing up, as every day was worse than the last. The ordeal put an unbelievable amount of stress and pressure on me, Maysa and my family—both close and extended—on a daily basis.

In the end, what I was left with was a very rude awakening. The Qatari legal system is the opposite of the United States legal system I grew up in. The U.S. concept of being innocent until proven guilty formed my frame of reference, and yet, the opposite is true in Qatar—you are considered guilty until proven innocent. The U.S. abolished debtor prisons in the nineteenth century, but they still exist in Qatar. In the U.S., you are not denied your freedom of movement because of a frivolous civil lawsuit, but in Qatar, any Qatari can place a ban on you from leaving the country for any number of meaningless reasons. In the U.S., it is common practice to incorporate to protect yourself from personal liability, and yet in Qatar, that same form of protection doesn't seem to exist. I was held personally responsible for wild allegations long after I was ceased being associated with the company.

I was forced to prove my innocence against blatant lies and unsubstantiated allegations by a minister, his brother, his aunt and cousins. I was denied the freedom to leave the country and held as an economic hostage, despite the fact that I had done nothing wrong, because the law afforded the locals that power. I was denied the right to work and earn a living for my family, not to mention to cover my own living expenses, for the majority of the time I was being held. To me, this is one of the most basic of human rights. I was at the mercy of morally corrupt individuals, and to this day, I must defend myself in a civil lawsuit because they continue to resort to frivolous allegations and stall tactics.

It's hard to say now, in retrospect, what I would have done differently, knowing what I know now. The short answer is that I wouldn't have gone. But the more complex answer is that this painful period of my life has led me down a path I would never have found had I not been exposed to the hardships I faced during my time trapped in Qatar.

I decided early on in my problems in Qatar—or should I say, I was forced to decide early on—that that in order to overcome this nightmare, I had to stand strong and resolute. I vowed that if I got out of that mess, I would do everything humanly possible to shed light on the injustices happening in the Gulf region.

Beginning immediately after regaining my freedom, I have dedicated a considerable amount of my time to this cause. This book is only the start in my fight to end the kafala, or sponsorship, system in this region.

Any country still using a sponsorship system should abolish the outdated practice. Qatar and other countries in the region are building their modern infrastructure and their new knowledge-based economies on the backs of hardworking expatriates of high rank and low. Those countries need the influx of foreign workers for their economies to continue to grow, but the leaders of those countries must learn to treat the foreign workers who are building their countries with respect and dignity. They must create rules and laws that protect the expatriates and treat them as equals to their own citizens.

While it may be hard for some to believe, in sponsorship systems, the foreign workers are treated as property—a system of modern day slavery. If the country finds that foreign workers are of value, they should treat them accordingly. The 21st century economy is a global market, and any country that desires to be a major player should play by the same rules as everyone else. Feudalism is dead.

In fact, the Arab Gulf can learn from America's history, where immigrants played a huge role in building a great nation. Today many immigrant groups are recognized and honored for their contributions; their stories can be found in the Arab American National Museum and other ethnic museums throughout the United States.

The Gulf nations, however, live and operate under the false premise that those who come to work for their benefit are in fact their indentured servants, in fact, disposable commodities. For this reason, those countries face a problem attracting and maintaining a talented, motivated workforce.

During my time in Qatar, it became quickly clear that foreign workers almost always feel that they are there to do their time and leave. The feeling of pride or ownership, in the sense of "owning" a success or achievement earned through hard and clever work— doesn't exist; it's not allowed to. But the problem is that you cannot have long-term sustainability with a short term workforce. When expatriates lack security, or worse, have a culture of fear forced upon them, this uneasiness is reflected in the achievements of these nations.

Compare the activity taking place in this region to the boomtowns that sprung up in the Western United States during the gold rush. Once the gold was gone, so too was the population; and the same will be true in the Gulf.

Sustainability is only derived when diverse economies are created. However, this is simply not feasible with small local populations. Only a steady influx of immigrants coming to these countries—immigrants who are able to stay, grow, and achieve much, because they are free to bring their families, achieve citizenship, and enjoy the rights afforded to other citizens—can achieve optimal results. These hard workers must have security and acceptance.

Our quest for stable and cheap energy should not entitle a country or region the privilege of enslaving guest workers, and the time to speak up is long overdue. The world has become too small. Facebook and Twitter have made it very transparent. Injustice has no place in a modern, educated society—the type that is projected by these Gulf countries. But appearances are deceiving.

I had the privileged connections and the financial means to fight and overcome this ordeal, but many, if not most others are not so fortunate. In fact, in the end, I found out my U.S. citizenship did not afford me certain underlying privileges that I would have expected. My government and embassy did the minimal to assist; it was actually my professional connections who were able to help the most. Others—from the Indian subcontinent, Middle East, Asia and Africa, may not be so lucky, and unfortunately for them, they are left with even less recourse or potential for justice to prevail in the end.

The kafala system employed in Qatar is as vile and illegitimate as apartheid. Western governments, corporations, educational initiations and civil societies need to act—now. Don't wait for the next big news story of an expatriate worker trapped in a foreign land for no good reason.

Until it cleans up its laws to be more in accordance with international standards, Qatar should not have the privilege to host any international events such as the FIFA World Cup, for its host venues, hotels and infrastructure are being built by slaves. Had FIFA picked the U.S., Australia, England or South Korea, these countries would have benefited from the economic bonanza, instead of a country that does not even provide basic human rights to its foreign workers. Yet FIFA picked Qatar, paving the way for a few privileged families to reap all the rewards. The bulk of the labor staff in Qatar, hailing from countries around the world, will toil for less than two hundred dollars a month to enable Qatar to shine on the international stage.

FIFA should have required any nation hosting the event to meet minimum international labor standards and norms. It should have been a requirement that was checked out and verified before the host country was named—before any country is even allowed to bid. But the corruption allegation against FIFA itself shows that the organization seems less interested in human rights and empowerment than domination of a sport and financial gain.

As an American, my DNA does not allow me to stand silent in the face of injustice. Too many Americans have fought and died for our freedom and the freedom of others. American-style capitalism means putting profits ahead of basic human rights, and the American consumer buys on the basis of price. We all need to give more thought to where our goods come from and re-think our priorities.

Americans as a people have an inherent tendency to root for the underdog. The dark-skinned men digging Doha's new highway interchanges in the midday sun are underdogs who have no right to howl. The slender Lebanese lady at a Doha reception desk is just as frightened of losing her position. The Filipino cleaning staff keep their mouths shut for a reason. And even the white-collar executives brought in because they have a track record of success are under-dogs in a legal framework that makes their employers their owners.

Martin Luther King taught us that, "Injustice anywhere is injustice everywhere." The people of the Arab Gulf have deep cultural mores guiding them in hosting guests. When will they apply these to guest workers? This is the proper way to treat those who have come to your shores to assist you in building your country.

Sponsorship is slavery, any way you dissect it. It needs to be abolished and the world must act. I believe that the American people will embrace this cause. The students at the universities that have a presence in the Gulf countries must be reviled by this archaic practice. The American consumer and shareholder will hold U.S. companies accountable for profiting from this immoral practice and insist that those Gulf governments change their oppressive ways. And the American Congress must act, for I am not the only American to endure this situation. Others are still being held throughout the Gulf.

One American, Zack Shahin, has been held in prison for four years in Dubai without a trial. His is far from the only other story out there. I have tried to ascertain from the U.S. State Department the number of Americans who are or have been victims of sponsorship abuse in the Gulf, but they won't even release the numbers. Again, whose interests are being served?

And more recently, Mohamed Bouazizi, the Tunisian street vendor who set himself on fire in protest of the confiscation of his wares and the harassment and humiliation that he reported was inflicted on him by a municipal official and her aides, became a catalyst for the Tunisian Revolution and the wider Arab Spring. His single act incited demonstrations and riots throughout region in protest of social and political issues and ensured that his suffering was not in vain. The public's anger and violence intensified following Bouazizi's death and led then-President Zine El Abidine Ben Ali to step down after 23 years in power. This very act had a domino effect that brought down the despots in Egypt, Libya and Yemen and forced political reform in Morocco. The ramifications of this singular act are still reverberating through the Middle East and beyond and as the dust settles, the outcomes will not produce positive change, if Qatar and Saudi Arabia use their abundant financial resources to instill hard-line Islamic regimes.

Qatar, as I have written, has been instrumental in supporting these democratic movements. But their motives are sinister; it is their way to deflect attention to their own lack of freedom and that of its Gulf neighbors. I doubt they would be taking such an aggressive role in the region without the blessing of the United States. One must then ask the question: what is our (as a nation) ultimate objections from the current political upheaval in the region. If I were a novice and optimist, I would think that America would want to see democracy blossom in the Arab World. However, that would entail seeking that same democratic change in our petrol allies in the Gulf. However, today's events clearly show our goals are to ensure that no Arab country challenge American influence and domination in the region, that we are willing to fan sectarian and religious differences to ensure continued political dominance of the Middle East. We will prop up absolute monarchies and provide them the military means to continue to subjugate their people to ensure an uninterrupted source of cheap oil. And the Arabs will play haplessly into this scenario. Change must come to this region, and an end to the archaic practice of sponsorship is a first step.

Appendix I: It Could Happen to You: Western Companies Operating in Qatar (And Why They Are)

While the oil and gas industries likely guarantee Qatar's ranking as one of the wealthiest countries in the world for some time to come and will support the country's economy, the kingdom led by Sheikh Hamad is aggressively preparing for a post-carbon world by seeking to stimulate the private sector and develop a knowledge-based economy.

These efforts are being undertaken using not only Qatar's own internal resources and human capital, but those of other countries as well. And not just any old intellectual property, research skills and ideas: Qatar is actively seeking—and screening for—the best of the best. These goals and pursuits have resulted in the development of several complex institutions to facilitate that growth that will be covered in this section.

In the past sixteen years since Sheikh Hamad seized power, and especially with Sheikha Mozah's active help, Qatar has opened its doors to Western, and particularly American, business expansion. The country is doing so through a number of ways, including establishing campuses to enable Qatari citizens to obtain an American degree, right in the oppressive desert heat of the Gulf; setting up tax-free havens to encourage the best and the brightest to set up their research facilities in Qatar to move Qatar's knowledge-based economy forward; and establishing a financial center that has quickly grown to serve as a regional powerhouse throughout the Gulf (and to a certain extent, the rest of the world, as it is attracting talent and resources from around the globe).

Access to ungodly amounts of cash can buy a lot, even a seemingly foolproof blueprint for a future economy to fall back on long after the oil wells have dried up. And that's exactly what Qatar is doing in its quest to develop a knowledge-based economy that will rival any of the best found in Europe or North America.

That's all fine and good. But these plans are executed at what cost to the foreign laborers being enticed to Qatar?

U.S. business expansion into Qatar, and to a greater extent, the expansion of global entities, has been somewhat limited in scope, with the majority of industries represented including oil/energy (obviously) as well as science and technology, research and development, finance and education. The education link is a seemingly odd collaboration between the two nations and definitely a first-of-its-kind endeavor that makes more sense after delving further into Qatar's motivations, which we will do in this appendix.

AMERICAN EDUCATION IN THE GULF DESERT

In what the *New York Times* called an "educational gold rush," American universities are competing to set up outposts in countries with limited higher education opportunities. And it's not just limited to American universities—Australian and British universities are starting, or expanding, hundreds of programs and partnerships in booming markets like China, India and Singapore.[106]

And, of course, Qatar.

Beyond programs and partnerships, some universities have gone as far as to set up full-fledged branch campuses, a still-new education model that greatly differs from traditional study abroad programs in its scope, reach and risks. Namely, this new model that Qatar purposefully internationally shopped for comes with big risks, including the reputation of the university setting up a branch campus.

To house these foreign branch campuses, the Qatar Foundation launched Education City in 1998, a 2,500 acre complex described as one of the world's first "multiversities," where participating universities share buildings and allow easy cross-registration among schools.

The benefit is twofold. Qatar is able to offer Qatari students (or students from other countries throughout the world) the chance to attend an American university without the expense, culture shock or post-9/11

---

106 Lewin, Tamar. "U.S. Universities Rush to Set Up Outposts Abroad." *The New York Times* 10 Feb. 2008

visa problems of traveling to America.[107] The universities setting up shop, on the other hand, get full financial backing from the Qatari government. In other words: a minimized risk, despite the fact that one could argue that they are being bought.

Located in the outskirts of Doha, Education City is the largest collection of American universities in the Middle East, with six American universities currently operating a branch location there. The universities are: Cornell's medical school, which combines pre-med training and professional training over six years; Virginia Commonwealth University's art and design program (which admitted women only for its first ten years of operation before it admitted men); Carnegie Mellon's computer and business programs; Texas A&M's engineering program; Georgetown's foreign service school; and Northwestern's journalism program.

But what's in it for the American universities, aside from being added to the Qatari bankroll? A lot, in theory. Satellite campuses can help universities raise their profile, build international relationships, attract top research talent (who, in turn, may attract grants and produce patents) and gain access to a new pool of tuition-paying students, just as the number of college-age Americans is about to decline.[108]

But the same article from the *New York Times* raised several important questions, some of which we may not be able to answer yet: Will the programs reflect American values and culture, or the host country's? Will American taxpayers end up footing part of the bill for overseas students (a.k.a. will Qatar ever stop its handouts)? What happens if relations between the United States and the host country deteriorate? And will foreign branches that spread American know-how hurt American competitiveness?

The universities started small. Even in 2008, over ten years after Education City was established, there were just 300 slots for new students for the following year's entering classes[109] among the five American universities in operation at the time.[110]

107 Lewin, Tamar. "U.S. Universities Rush to Set Up Outposts Abroad." *The New York Times* 10 Feb. 2008

108 Lewin, Tamar. "U.S. Universities Rush to Set Up Outposts Abroad." *The New York Times* 10 Feb. 2008

109 Lewin, Tamar. "In Oil-Rich Mideast, Shades of the Ivy League." *The New York Times* 11 Feb. 2008

110 Lewin, Tamar. "In Oil-Rich Mideast, Shades of the Ivy League." *The New York Times* 11 Feb. 2008

Northwestern University in Qatar began degree programs in journalism and communication in fall 2008. There is also one Qatari university, Qatar Faculty of Islamic Studies, which began in 2007 by offering a Masters degree in Islamic Studies. In 2011 one French University, HEC Paris, and one British university, UCL Qatar, also began operating in the Education City complex. HEC Paris is the first to offer executive education programs in Qatar, including an international Executive MBA, and UCL Qatar offers postgraduate degree programs in Archaeology, Conservation, Cultural Heritage and Museum Studies.

Other schools spent time considering opening an Education City campus before abandoning the idea, including the University of North Carolina, which gave up for financial reasons; the University of Virginia, which pulled out over concerns it could not meet accreditation requirements; and the University of Texas decided it would detract from its mission in Austin.[111]

But it's big money for the American universities. To ensure the project's success, Qatar has guaranteed there will be no financial risk to the universities. During the construction phase, Qatar brought in cutting-edge architects to complete construction of the facilities. For the Cornell medical school alone, the Qatar Foundation promised $750 million over 11 years.[112] In general, Qatar pays for the architecturally stunning classroom buildings, the faculty salaries and housing and transportation, and it has made multimillion-dollar gifts to the other Education City universities.[113]

Today Education City is home to 1,300 students of 70 nationalities (although about half are Qatari). Students apply to the particular school they wish to attend; however, there is an odd sense of easy collaboration among the institutions not seen very often in the U.S. Once admitted, students are permitted to cross-register and take classes from different institutions. The student's "main" university will accept the transfer of credits as if the class were its own.

Sheikha Mozah has said she and Sheikh Hamad toured dozens of institutions around the world before settling on the U.S. style of university

---

111   "Education City: A Radical Experiment in Education: American Universities in the Middle East." *Now* 16 May 2008

112   Lewin, Tamar. "In Oil-Rich Mideast, Shades of the Ivy League." *The New York Times* 11 Feb. 2008

113   Lewin, Tamar. "In Oil-Rich Mideast, Shades of the Ivy League." *The New York Times* 11 Feb. 2008

education. Price was no object in the quest for quality. Apparently so, because investment in the project is in the billions of dollars.[114]

Interestingly, due to the amount of money Qatar was willing and able to spend on the development of the project, most of the facilities in Education City are far ahead of the universities' counterparts in the U.S.

RESEARCH & DEVELOPMENT TO BOLSTER QATAR'S KNOWLEDGE-BASED ECONOMY

The U.S. is the major equipment supplier for Qatar's oil and gas industry, and U.S. companies are playing a major role in the development of the oil and gas sector and petrochemicals. Qatar has made it easy for foreign companies to develop their technologies through its Science and Technology Park (QSTP), which operates under the objective to attract companies and entrepreneurs from around the world to commercialize their technologies in Qatar.

For Qatar, the goal behind the science and technology park is to spur the development of Qatar's knowledge economy, in an attempt to move to a post-carbon world (in other words, the country is looking to not miss a beat when we are forced to transition away from oil and gas).

The QSTP website details some of the benefits companies choosing to locate there will receive. It promises "world-class offices and laboratories specifically designed for technology-based companies" paid for by the $600 million the Qatar Foundation has invested in its first phase of buildings. Companies can lease in the already-existing multi-user buildings or commission their own buildings for design and build by QSTP (to be leased back). Members are not given the office space for free (which is somewhat of a surprise, in comparison to the Education City facility), but the rent tenants do pay is reported to be competitive with other commercial Doha prices (although rates are not published). QSTP says the advantage of its own facilities stem from the research-grade specification of its buildings and infrastructure.

Otherwise, there are many advantages to setting up a business in QSTP over a general commercial space in Doha; perhaps the greatest of which is that it's a tax-free zone. The complex in general operates as a free-trade zone to make it easy for foreign companies to set up shop

---

114 Mendenhall, Preston. "U.S. Education Takes Root in Arab Desert: Qatar Transforms Desert Land into Center for Learning, Tolerance." *MSNBC* 21 Feb. 2005

without dealing with the pesky Qatari laws that make it to difficult (and dangerous) to everyone else.

The Qatar Foundation seems to have pulled out all the stops to make the QSTP a success. Easy access to research institutes is one of the main considerations for an R&D-intensive company to select a location. In 2006 Georgia Tech surveyed 249 R&D-intensive companies on how they chose where to do their research. The answer was that their decision was "most influenced by the ease of collaboration with nearby universities and the presence of faculty with special expertise."

And conveniently, QSTP is able to tout its location within Education City as one of its advantages.

Funding is also available to member companies, in limited amounts (well, relatively limited, compared to other Qatari initiatives). The New Enterprise Fund provides capital for start-up technology companies locating at Qatar Science & Technology Park. The $30 million fund makes equity investments ranging from $500,000 to $3 million in start-up companies at the science park, from the seed stage through to the early growth stage.

Some of QSTP's more recognizable members include Chevron, Cisco, ConocoPhillips, ExxonMobil, GE, Microsoft, Rolls Royce, and Shell.

Gulf Times reported on some of QSTP's successes thus far, as reported by Dr. Tidu Maini, executive chairman of Qatar Science and Technology Park, including QSTP's solar power demonstrator and testing facilities, their geosciences research efforts in partnership with Shell and Qatar Petroleum (which is looking at exploiting empty reservoirs and using CO_2 to extract remaining resources), and their composite materials research, which has come about through Qatar's acquisition of 20% of Porsche Volkswagen. The technology transfer that was part of the Porsche Volkswagen deal allows Qatar to exploit its advantage in hydrocarbon resources to develop new industries in the country.[115]

The article also reported that QSTP's research has produced results in the motorcycle industry and healthcare. Qatari developers have also created a platform using existing technology that can take inputs in text, speech or video in a variety of languages and automatically translate them. Maini said that the system, called Loghati (Arabic for 'My language') is currently being adopted at MIT in Massachusetts and in Italy, and is an

---

115 "No Development without Innovation." *Gulf Times* 25 Apr. 2012

example of how finding gaps in the market can, in a very short time, turn into exports for the 'Made in Qatar' brand.[116]

Interestingly, as reported in the Daily Energy Report, the U.S. Department of Energy has also teamed up with Qatar for clean energy. The DOE is reportedly working with the QSTP under an agreement to promote clean energy. Both countries will exchange innovations and take part in joint research initiatives to garner economic growth. The collaboration will focus on five areas: advanced cooling technologies, renewable power generation, energy storage, carbon capture and water treatment systems.[117]

ExxonMobil: An American Behemoth in Qatar

For a deeper look at one of QSTP's anchor members, we can look to ExxonMobil, which has had a decades-long history of partnering with and investing in Qatar, to assist the country in its efforts to export liquefied natural gas.

In a feature about the partnership between ExxonMobil and Qatar, the National U.S.-Arab Chamber of Commerce writes that ExxonMobil's "commitment to Qatar extends beyond that of a joint venture partner and investor. The company is active in a variety of initiatives and projects to support economic growth and the wellbeing of Qatar. ExxonMobil also strives to uphold the Four Pillars of Qatar's National Vision 2030 – human, social, economic, and environmental development. The company shares the Qatar Foundation's objectives to advance science and technology through research and development. ExxonMobil Research Qatar Limited is an anchor tenant at the Qatar Science & Technology Park in Doha."

A Growing Financial Services Sector

QSTP is not the only active free-trade zone in Qatar; the Qatar Financial Centre (QFC) is located in Doha and is designed to attract international financial institutions and multinational corporations to participate in Qatar's growing market for financial services and establish operations in a "best-in-class" business and legal environment.

The QFC Authority is responsible for leading the expansion of Qatar's financial services sector and for developing relationships with the

---

116   "No Development without Innovation." *Gulf Times* 25 Apr. 2012
117   "Study: Biofuel Production Predicted to Increase." *Daily Energy Report* Apr. 2011

regional and global financial community. In February 2010 the QFC Authority unveiled a new strategy focusing on the creation of a global business hub for three core markets: Asset Management, Reinsurance and Captive Insurance.

The QFC provides Qatari and international firms with access to local and regional investment opportunities, including over US$137 billion of prospective infrastructure investment in Qatar through to 2015, as well as over US$1.2 trillion of planned investment across the GCC.

The QFC website reports that 140 licenses have been issued to both international and domestic firms, including well-known financial services firms such as AIG/Alico, Allianz, AXA, Barclays Capital, Citibank, Credit Suisse, Deutsche Bank, ICBC, JP Morgan, Kane, KPMG, Marsh, Mitsui Sumitomo, Morgan Stanley, PricewaterhouseCoopers, UBS and Zurich FS.

According to a case study by Wolf Olins, a brand consultancy firm that formed an integrated team with a PR and an advertising agency to develop a brand and marketing program for the financial centre, the Qatari Minister of Economy and Commerce said in 2007: 'Within the space of just two years the QFC has reached a stage of maturity that many of the world's more established centers took years or even decades to achieve.' The QFC witnessed a dramatic 82% increase in income at the end of its first fully operational year. In 2008 the QFC achieved the landmark of authorizing the application of its 100th firm. The QFC's income has grown at an average rate of 42% per year, reaching $2.3 million in 2008.

Today the Qatar Financial Center Authority operates a significant loan service to the region, offering $1.2 trillion of funds towards supporting development projects across the GCC region.[118]

Further, the Qatar Stock Exchange has announced the creation of a smaller exchange, the "QE Venture Market," specifically designed to cater for and support SMEs, as part of Qatar's desire to promote SMEs as an important contributor to the economy and strengthen the private sector in Qatar. It has also recently been announced that a new market for companies incorporated in the Qatar Financial Center will be established as part of the Qatar Exchange before the end of the year.

Interestingly, both the QFC and QSTP have their own immigration and employment laws and are exempt from normal Qatari sponsorship laws. An article by *Euromoney* indicates the Qatar Financial Center has been promoted as operating under a "mostly British-inspired financial

---

118 "GCC in the Driving Seat." *World Finance* 23 Apr. 2012

legal system as an alternative to Qatar's Islamic Shari'a-based law." The article goes on to say that "some lawyers say its very creation suggests the Qataris know their traditional legal system is ill-equipped for a modern financial services center."[119]

So it is apparent that the Qatari government is aware of its own unjust system and took steps to correct it—but only for the privileged few who are making great strides in building Qatar's knowledge-based economy (not the ones actually building the offices in which they sit).

RUMORS OF CORRUPTION AND THE DANGER TO FOREIGN WORKERS

The *Economic Times* reported that Saleh Bin Saad al-Mana, the Vice-President of Government and Public Affairs at ExxonMobil, Qatar, said ExxonMobil Qatar's investments in Qatar might exceed $16 billion over the next five years, compared to a world total of $37 billion.[120]

However, news reports have indicated that relations between Qatar and international companies have not always been so straightforward and positive-seeming.

In 2011 British paper *The Telegraph* reported that leaked diplomatic cables indicated that Qatar wrote to major international oil companies, including Royal Dutch Shell and ExxonMobil, to demand up to $1.7 billion in donations for a medical center.

The article says according to the Wikileaks documents, "letters signed by Abdullah al-Attiyah, the deputy prime minister, told each company how much they were expected to donate."[121]

Figures ranged from $280 million for Exxon to $80 million for Total.

The article went on to say that other companies said to have been approached were ConocoPhillips, Occidental, Q-Chem, Microsoft and General Electric.

"In the diplomatic documents obtained by Reuters, U.S. officials viewed the requests as a 'bad miscalculation' by the country's energy ministry and Sheikha Mozah bint Nasser al-Missned, wife of Qatar's ruler.

---

119   Ellis, Eric. "David Proctor: The Banker Who Can't Get Out of Qatar." *Euromoney* Jan. 2010

120   "ExxonMobil to Invest $16 bn in Qatar Over Next 5 Years." *The Economic Times* 23 May 2011

121   Mason, Rowena. "Qatar Asked Shell and ExxonMobil for Donations." *The Telegraph* 22 Mar. 2011

"'The IOCs [international oil companies] are shocked and angered by the request,' the cable stated.[122]

Without a doubt, this book could report on other alleged scandals, as well as other tidbits of good news of collaboration elaborately weaved by a PR machine, but my point in reporting on the excessively tempting lure of Qatar is that many of these workers will face dangers they cannot imagine, and dream jobs can turn into nightmares.

It is simply not enough for Qatar to "look the other way" or bend the rules for a small percentage of elite white-collar workers coming to work within the Qatar Financial Center's protective walls; the country needs to reform its labor laws for all foreign workers entering its borders.

---

122 Mason, Rowena. "Qatar Asked Shell and ExxonMobil for Donations." *The Telegraph* 22 Mar. 2011

Appendix II: Other Westerners Trapped in Qatar

Unfortunately my story is not unique; there are countless stories of expatriates unable to leave Qatar, so many so that a phrase has been coined to describe the phenomenon: going to China.

The slang term for being held hostage in Qatar is perhaps intentionally vague, and many expatriates are not willing to publicly discuss the injustices they hear about, anyway; they fear they may be next. Below are a few stories, some better known than others, of people who found themselves in similar predicaments in Qatar. Know that these few examples, while shedding a better light on the injustices, are hardly even scratching the surface.

David Proctor

Originally headhunted to run a startup bank in Doha in 2007, just over two years later David Proctor became known as "the banker who can't get out of Qatar."

Proctor, a British citizen, came to Qatar with an impressive resume. He has a Cambridge degree and came with twenty-five years of experience, including having served as regional CEO of Bank of America in Thailand and regional CEO of Standard Chartered Bank in Europe and the Middle East.

So when the new bank called Al-Khaliji made their offer, Proctor came to the position with a great deal of experience and prestige. When he arrived, the bank had just five employees and no systems or customers yet in place, but a clear mission to build a strong bank across the Gulf (the name is the Arabic term for "the Gulf").

Over the course of the next two years, Proctor worked to grow the bank across the region, and under Proctor's leadership, Al-Khaliji was profitable and even "outmaneuvered" the established Qatar National Bank in several significant deals in Doha, Dubai and Paris.[123]

In a TV interview with Bloomberg following his eventual release, Proctor speculated that his detention was due to the "changing political winds in Qatar." He noted that at the end of 2008, Al-Khaliji had purchased a bank that was highly coveted by some of their competitors, giving them licenses in Europe and a branch network in the UAE. Two months after that acquisition, the previous vice chairman of Qatar National Bank, one of their biggest competitors, and a member of the royal family, was appointed as Proctor's new chairman.[124]

That was when things began to change for Proctor. The chairman who had recruited him was gone, and Proctor felt it was time to part ways, so he gave his notice.

A *Euromoney* article published in January 2010 said Proctor negotiated his exit terms, and "there was nothing to suggest anything was irregular or untoward, but the paperwork simply didn't arrive as promised. Far from paying him a severance and bidding him farewell, Al-Khaliji's new chairman... has refused to not only pay what was agreed to Proctor, he has also refused him permission to leave."[125]

While Proctor waited for an exit permit to materialize, other expatriates previously on Proctor's team faced trouble as well. His head of IT, Steve Shipley, had to pay back his $500,000 sign-on fee before his passport was stamped with an exit visa.[126] Proctor himself offered to pay back various fees and bonuses in exchange for his exit permit, but his offers were always ignored.

Proctor maintained his innocence of any wrongdoings; and supportive of his claim, there were never any legal proceedings against him.

123 Ellis, Eric. "'Nightmare Over' for UK Banker Held in Qatar." *Euromoney* 30 Apr. 2010

124 "Proctor Discusses Experience in Qatar." *Bloomberg TV* 17 May 2011

125 Ellis, Eric. "David Proctor: The Banker Who Can't Get Out of Qatar." *Euromoney* Jan. 2010

126 Ellis, Eric. "David Proctor: The Banker Who Can't Get Out of Qatar." *Euromoney* Jan. 2010

The same article said, "the British government said they were advised by Qatar's attorney-general that Proctor has no legal case to answer in Qatar."[127]

In fact, Proctor himself never had a clear idea of why he was stuck in legal purgatory—he was never questioned by police or Qatar's public prosecutor—and in the end, it took Proctor fourteen months to get his exit permit. Proctor cites the 2010 article published in *Euromoney* as what ultimately helped raise awareness of his case and allow him to leave Qatar.

PHILIPPE BOGAERT

Philippe Bogaert is a Belgian who moved to Qatar in April of 2008 to work for the local subsidiary of a Belgian company, Dialogic, as a media specialist to develop media coverage of the Qatar Marine Festival. The festival is an annual major cultural event that the Qatari government produces to promote the Emirate's cultural attractions.

Bogaert had previously worked for the parent company in Belgium. Prior to arriving in Qatar, he had no awareness of the dangers of Qatar's work sponsorship system.

By email, Bogaert told me he wasn't even informed about the sponsorship system—it had been "taken care of" by his company.

Shortly before he arrived in Qatar, the relationship between Dialogic Qatar and the festival organizing committee had soured. Dialogic claimed the festival organizing committee owed it several million Qatari riyals. The company's existing managing director was fired, and Bogaert, because he was well known and trusted by the Belgian headquarters, was asked to run the company.

Bogaert notes that responsibility equals danger in Qatar.

"From the moment I took over as managing director, a job I accepted with the mission to put the troubled company back on track, the dream job turned into a nightmare," Bogaert said.

He was tasked with salvaging its relationship with the company's only client—the festival committee. But efforts were not successful, and with no cashflow, the group decided against pursing the festival organizers for the cash owed. Bogaert focused on trying to liquidate the company, and he began looking forward to going home to his wife and children.

---

127 Ellis, Eric. "David Proctor: The Banker Who Can't Get Out of Qatar." *Euromoney* Jan. 2010

However, when Dialogic Qatar was formed, a 51 percent stake was given to Farukh Mohammad Azad, a Pakistan-born Qatari national who had worked with Dialogic on other events in the Gulf state.

Azad was considered a vital contact with Qatari authorities, but he pulled out of the contract and Dialogic Qatar went bankrupt. Bogaert resigned, and his resignation was accepted by the Belgian parent company, Dialogic SA, but Azad refused to sign Bogaert's exit permit, preventing him from leaving Qatar indefinitely. This also meant Bogaert had no job and no income, as he was not allowed to work for anyone else.

Bogaert said that when he took the position he was unaware of the size and real nature of the trouble with the company and pre-existing issues with payment. While trapped in Qatar, he speculated that his sponsor was concerned that he would be held responsible for the debts himself, plus any fees demanded to be returned for the "unfulfilled" contract (under Qatari law, a sponsor may be held liable for such debt).

He had tried multiple times to get out of the country, yet every time he had been blocked. Finally, some friends suggested he try to raise awareness about his story through Twitter and a blog.

"This is the story of how I became a prisoner in Qatar. Consider it my Twitter SOS," reads his first tweet as @hostageinqatar.

The next several tweets sum up his predicament:

In 2008, I was offered my dream job. A company I had worked for in Belgium, Dialogic, was looking for a broadcast manager in Qatar.

I would be working with The Qatar Marine Festival. It was a great challenge, an opportunity to work internationally.

Sheikha Mozah, the Emir's wife, was behind the festival. She is a very cool woman.

I was fascinated by the chance to work in an exotic Kingdom on an exciting project. In retrospect, I might have been a bit naïve.

But how could I have imagined that I would soon be a prisoner, far from my family, caught in a drama reminiscent of Kafka's Trial?

For over a year in Qatar, Bogaert had no income and no way of leaving. He was lucky enough to be allowed to live in the Belgian ambassador's residence after his apartment lease ran out.

Bogaert's Twitter feed details his story in tiny, digestible nuggets. Here's the part about what happened when his lease expired and he had no money for another one:

Stranded, out of cash, I packed my luggage and went to the Belgium Embassy in Qatar in early December.

"Send me home," I pleaded.

"Sorry, can't send you back to Belgium," said the ambassador. He offered me a loan so I could pay for a hotel room.

If you have any idea how expensive hotels are in Qatar, you'll know why I refused his offer.

So he allowed me to stay at his personal residence. That's where I am twittering right now, six months later, still held hostage in Qatar.

To support myself, I'm falling back on an old talent. I'm playing the piano and singing in bars and restaurants around Doha.

Bogaert expressed his gratitude at the ambassador's generosity, and yet, the ambassador could only help so much.

"Apart from bed and breakfast, even though the ambassador served as a door-opener with key personalities and lawyers, diplomacy wasn't able to force any breakthrough," Bogaert said. "It must be said that large economic interests must prevail over one person's problem..."

Bogaert noted that the use of media did bring more attention to his case, but it also got him into "exponentially bigger problems," including a 10 million euro court case for defamation.

"That's when I realized I had to get out," he said.

In the end, he managed to escape by sea in a story worthy of Hollywood.

He is unsure as to whether all the charges have been dropped, but he did know that he won all the cases for which he was able to pay a lawyer and defend himself.

Other Victims

Ian Heywood

Euromoney also reported on Qatar Airways executive Ian Heywood, who was unable to leave Qatar for much of 2008. He had been headhunted for a job at a British airline following a year in Doha with Qatar Airways. During his notice period in 2008, he was detained by Qatari police as he was boarding a return flight for a business trip to Bahrain. He was held in solitary confinement for over a month until finally a "breach of contract" was brought against him by Qatar Airways. Six months later it was thrown out after a brief hearing, but at that point, the BMI job waiting for him had been filled.[128]

Tracy Edwards

The same article reports on Tracy Edwards, the world champion British yachtswoman who, after a $15 million deal with the al-Thanis to promote Qatar as an international yachting center (warning: don't forget the sunblock) went sour, wasn't able to leave Qatar for a month.[129]

Yves Pendeliau

And, of course, there are countless others still trapped in Qatar who have not managed to have their travel bans lifted. Yves Pendeliau is a French citizen currently trapped in Qatar due to a travel ban issued without notification in July of 2011. The ban is related to an apartment rental dispute that arose from a change in ownership of the apartment complex. Pendeliau says the ban requires payment of nearly QR 50,000, and there is no guarantee he will be free after having paid the amount.

Pendeliau calls the demands basic extortion. "A translation of the court document indicated that I was under travel ban without a court case. Consequently, the case will never be judged in court," Pendeliau said.

Pendeliau previously worked for Shell in Qatar. He is currently separated from his wife and three children because of this ordeal.

---

128 Ellis, Eric. "David Proctor: The Banker Who Can't Get Out of Qatar." *Euromoney* Jan. 2010

129 Ellis, Eric. "David Proctor: The Banker Who Can't Get Out of Qatar." *Euromoney* Jan. 2010

Appendix III: Advice to Americans Looking to Work Abroad

Today's global economy means more and more people are accepting work overseas. There are many benefits to accepting a job in a foreign country, including developing intercultural communication skills, enhancing interpersonal skills, and developing an international network of colleagues. Additionally, you will have the chance to be exposed to a variety of organizational structures and see how culture influences the workplace in other countries, and ideally, you will be able to use this understanding to strengthen your own career path, whether you plan to stay overseas or return to the United States.

However, many people accept jobs overseas without giving thorough consideration to the implications of life in a specific foreign country.

Before any serious consideration is given to accepting a job overseas, it is important to research entry and visa requirements for the country. The U.S. State Department website offers a wealth of information. Additionally, it is recommended that you check with the IRS website to investigate tax requirements, and also learn about tax laws in the country you are considering working in (consult an expert who is familiar with tax laws). The country you are considering working in may very well have laws you are not familiar with or would not expect. For example, when you buy a television in the United Kingdom, you pay a yearly tax that goes toward public television. Taxes on income will vary with each situation, but it is imperative to understand the details before accepting a position. Otherwise, you risk returning home a few years later with a large tax bill or paying tax to two countries while working overseas.

It is also important to picture the cultural and social differences you may face, particularly in a nation with vastly different values and traditions, and consider how comfortable you will be. In addition to any social differences in day-to-day life, there may be vast differences in workplace settings and behaviors that may take quite a bit of adjustment. To get an objective sense of whether you have the personality required to deal with these challenges overseas, seek advice and honest feedback from people who have worked with you in the past. Their input will assist you in understanding any areas you will need to develop in order to make your transition a success.

Generally, to obtain resident and legal work status in a country, a few things must be in place: you must already have a job waiting for you, you must have the means to live for some time without working, you must fulfill government criteria to establish a business, and/or you must be descended from or married to a national. Certain organizations can help obtain a temporary work visa, depending on the country you are going to. Once you have a temporary work visa, it would be up to the employing company to sponsor you for longer.

If you ultimately get a job offer from a fairly well known international company, there may be less to be cautious of than if you are considering an offer from a smaller, relatively unknown company that operates only in that country. It may be worthwhile to first speak to the American Embassy closest to the city the potential employer is located in. Employees at the embassy may be able to offer additional insight about the company, including whether other Americans have encountered problems with the company in the past.

Most important, you need to have a vital understanding of the contract you are entering into and the terms, benefits and bonuses that will be applied. Understand whether it's a local contract, where you will be bound by all the employment laws of the host country or an international contract, where you might enjoy some expat benefits or additional protection. It is equally important to understand what happens when the contract ends or if it is terminated early by you or the employer. Will you be offered a repatriation package? What are the other severance details and notice periods required? Always make sure you have everything in writing. Verbal agreements don't offer the same kind of protection that written ones do.

Networking is also crucial. Reach out to all your contacts to find out if they know anyone in the area you are considering moving to, and talk to as many people as you can in that city, especially other expatriate workers, if possible. Make a point to meet with them in person soon after you move, as well.

Learn as much as you can about the country's legal system and social customs. In Qatar, it appears to be the norm that you are "guilty until proven innocent," which is obviously a far cry from what we are used to here in the U.S.

Take some time to understand the local economy. If you're going to be paid in that country's currency, find out what their quality of life is like and what the cost of living is. Investigate whether you'll receive any tax breaks, whether housing and transportation will be covered, or what other financial incentives are being offered.

Also take some time to learn about the local history and traditions. The knowledge will go a long way in understanding the region and its people and making friends.

If you are planning on bringing family with you, there are an additional set of concerns that should be addressed. Is the area safe for them? Will your children be able to adjust easily? Are there any American or International schools nearby that they will be able to attend? Will your new company cover the cost of their tuition? Will the government permit your spouse to work, and if so, will he or she have an easy time finding a job? What about childcare? Spend some time considering the impact living abroad will have on your children and your partner. Although a move overseas may advance your own career, how will it impact the long-term prospects of other family members? What social opportunities are available for members of your family? These are all important factors in making your decision. Additionally, think about the family members you are leaving behind. Will the age and health of your parents or other family members be a factor? Will there be someone to care for them in the event of illness? How often will you be allowed to visit home, and will any of your travel expenses be covered?

It is also important to give some consideration to your long term goals. If you will ultimately be returning to the U.S., how do you plan to reenter the U.S. market? Will your skills be obsolete or enhanced by your sojourn abroad? How easily will you be able to keep in touch with important contacts who are still in the U.S. and keep abreast of developments in your field? What will your job security be like in your role overseas? If your job is made redundant for any reason, what will happen then?

Finally, it is very easy to become homesick or depressed. Make sure your expectations and assumptions are in check. It's easy for an experience to fall short if you've already got it fully mapped out in your head.

ACKNOWLEDGEMENTS

I dedicate this book to my wonderful wife Maysa for her support, love and belief in me. She was the rock when I wobbled. To my three wonderful children, Aya, Jana and Mohamad Jamal: every day I was trapped in Qatar I thought of them and longed to be with them, and that got me through. To the family, friends and colleagues whose support never wavered, who sometimes put themselves in peril to assist me. They were there when we needed them and helped us overcome this traumatic ordeal.

The unexpected benefit of being trapped in a foreign country is that it allows you to formulate an accurate picture of people you thought you knew. Ironically, those I had a relationship with and had assisted and supported over the years and considered my friends did nothing. Instead, I found out who my biggest supporters were—the people who had nothing to gain yet helped anyway, because they are genuinely good people. As long as there are warm and caring people in the world, there is hope, and I cannot express in words my appreciation for the moral support they showed Maysa and me.

And I would be remiss to not offer my thanks as well to the cigars, whose smoking pleasure provided hours of enjoyment, tranquility and inspiration while beginning to write this book on the Pearl Island in Qatar, unsure of when I would be coming home, and also as I finished writing it, happy to have an ending to my story, at Casa De Habana in Detroit.

BIBLIOGRAPHY

AFP. "Qatar Pledges $10 bln Investment in Egypt." 28 May 2011.

AFP. "Qatar Pledges to Invest $2 bn in Sudan." 7 Mar. 2012.

Al Jazeera. "Qatar Withdraws from Yemen Mediation Bid." 13 May 2011.

Associated Press. "A Look at How Egypt's Uprising Unfolded." 11 Feb. 2011.

Azouz, Mohamed. "Qatar Supports Egypt's General Budget with US$500 Million, Increases Investments." *Egypt Independent* 6 Oct. 2011.

BBC. "Sudan Profile." 1 May 2012.

BBC. "Why is Qatar Buying Up London Landmarks?" 1 May 2011.

Beaumont, Peter. "Qatar Accused of Interfering in Libyan Affairs." *The Guardian* 4 Oct. 2011.

Black, Ian. "Qatar Admits Sending Hundreds of Troops to Support Libya Rebels." *The Guardian* 26 Oct. 2011.

Bloomberg TV. "Proctor Discusses Experience in Qatar." 17 May 2011.

Booth, Robert. "WikiLeaks Cables Claim al-Jazeera Changed Coverage to Suit Qatari Foreign Policy." *The Guardian* 5 Dec. 2010.

Buchanan, Michael. "Qatar Flexing Muscle in Changing World." *BBC News* 28 Dec. 2011.

CNN. "Qatar Bails out of Yemen Pact, Citing 'Procrastination'." 12 May 2011.

CNN. "Sudan's Defense Minister Wanted for War Crimes." 2 Mar. 2012.

CNN. "Timeline: Decades of Conflict in Lebanon, Israel." 14 Jul. 2006.

Cockburn, Patrick. "Emir of Qatar deposed by his son." *The Independent* 28 Jun. 1995.

Consulate General of the State of Qatar, The. "Egyptian FM Hails Qatar's Role in Darfur Peace Process." 14 July 2011.

Daily Energy Report. "Study: Biofuel Production Predicted to Increase." Apr. 2011.

Daily Mail Online. "Qatar World Cup stadium designer tells 2022 hosts air conditioned stadiums must be scrapped." 8 Nov. 2011

Daily Star, The. "Lebanon, Qatar Discuss Boosting Bilateral Cooperation." 6 Mar. 2012.

Dickinson, Elizabeth. "Qatar Builds Brand as Mediator." *The Christian Science Monitor* 28 Mar. 2012.

Dietz, David. "How Qatar Rose to Become a Leading Player in Middle East Politics." *Policymic* Jan. 2012.

Eakin, Hugh. "The Strange Power of Qatar." *The New York Review of Books* 27 Oct. 2011.

Economic Times, The. "ExxonMobil to Invest $16 bn in Qatar Over Next 5 Years." 23 May 2011.

Education for Development Magazine. "Sponsorship System and its Effects on Expatriate Workers in the Gulf Cooperation Council (GCC) Countries." 28 Dec. 2009.

El Ghanem, Nasser. "Qatar Considers Review of Sponsorship Law." *Al-Shorfa* 11 Jan. 2011.

Ellis, Eric. "'Nightmare Over' for UK Banker Held in Qatar." *Euromoney* 30 Apr. 2010.

Ellis, Eric. "David Proctor: The Banker Who Can't Get Out of Qatar." *Euromoney* Jan. 2010.

Elshamy, Anwar. "Dream Comes True for Qatar's First Woman Judge." *Gulf Times* 17 Mar. 2010.

Eshelby, Kate. "Tunisia: A Year on from the Revolution." *The Metro* 6 Mar. 2012.

Evans, Dominic. "One Year On, Syria's Assad won't Bow to Uprising." *Reuters* 14 Mar. 2012.

Financial Times, The. "Qatar Pulls out of Yemen Crisis Mediation." 13 May 2011.

Freedom House. "Women's Rights in the Middle East and North Africa – Qatar." 14 Oct. 2005.

Fromhertz, Allen J. *Qatar: A Modern History*. Washington D.C., Georgetown University Press. 15 Feb. 2012.

Green, R. "Solving the Darfur Crisis: The U.S. Prefers Qatar to Egypt as Mediator." *The Middle East Media Research Institute* 19 Aug. 2009.

Gulf Times. "No Development without Innovation." 25 Apr. 2012.

Gulf Times. "Qatar, Tunisia Sign Investment Accords." 14 Jan. 2012.

Gulf Times. "Sponsorship System Studies 'Delayed'." 13 Mar. 2011.

Harmassi, Mohammed. "Bahrain to End 'Slavery' System." *BBC* 6 May 2009.

Huffington Post, The. "World's Most Water Stressed Countries: Bahrain, Qatar, Yemen Facing Extreme Shortages." 19 May 2011.

Irish, John. "France's Le Pen Attacks Qatar, Fears Islamist Threat." *Reuters* 13 Jan. 2012.

Jackson, David. "Obama: 'No Big Move Toward Democracy in Qatar'." *USA Today* 16 Apr. 2011.

Khaleej Times. "Doha Forum Highlights Reforms in the Arab World." 9 May 2011.

Kiefer, Francine. "Qatar: The Small Arab Monarchy with the Loud Democratic Voice." *The Christian Science Monitor* 27 May 2011.

Lewin, Tamar. "In Oil-Rich Mideast, Shades of the Ivy League." *The New York Times* 11 Feb. 2008.

Lewin, Tamar. "U.S. Universities Rush to Set Up Outposts Abroad." *The New York Times* 10 Feb. 2008.

Los Angeles Times. "Lebanon: Qatar Emerges as Diplomatic Powerhouse." 15 May 2008.

Los Angeles Times. "Yemen: Qatar Withdraws Support for GCC Agreement; Expert Warns of Violence." 13 May 2011.

Mason, Rowena. "Qatar Asked Shell and ExxonMobil for Donations." *The Telegraph* 22 Mar. 2011.

McKelvey, Tara. "In Arabic in English in D.C." *The American Prospect* 17 Dec. 2006.

Mendenhall, Preston. "U.S. Education Takes Root in Arab Desert: Qatar Transforms Desert Land into Center for Learning, Tolerance." *MSNBC* 21 Feb. 2005.

Middle East Online. "Deciphering the Qatar Enigma." 28 Feb. 2012.

Noe, Nicholas and Raad, Walid. "Al-Jazeera Gets Rap as Qatar Mouthpiece." *Bloomberg* 9 Apr. 2012.

Now. "Education City: A Radical Experiment in Education: American Universities in the Middle East." 16 May 2008.

Peninsula, The. "Qatar tops per capita water use in world." 30 Mar. 2011.

Peninsula, The. "QCCI Wants Sponsorship, Exit Permits to Continue." 11 Oct. 2010.

Pintak, Lawrence. "The Al Jazeera Revolution." *Foreign Policy* 2 Feb. 2011.

Reuters Africa. "Egypt says Qatar Gave $500 mln to Help with Budget." 9 Oct. 2011.

Reuters Africa. "Qatar Presses Yemen's Saleh on Power Transfer Deal." 17 Nov. 2011.

Reuters. "Qatar Presses Yemen's Saleh on Power Transfer Deal." 17 Nov. 2011.

Roberts, David. "Behind Qatar's Intervention in Libya." *Foreign Affairs* 28 Sept. 2011.

Sambidge, Andy. "Salary Delay is No 1 Worker Complaint in Qatar in Q1." *Arabian Business* 23 Jun. 2010.

Shadid, Anthony. "Qatar Wields an Outsize Influence in Arab Politics." *The New York Times* 14 Nov. 2011.

Shahine, Alaa. "Tunisia May Sell Debt to Qatar, Needs $5 Billion Financing." *Bloomberg* 27 Jan. 2012.

Smoltczyk, Alexander and Zand, Bernhard. "Tiny Qatar has Big Diplomatic Ambitions." *Der Spiegel* 14 Mar. 2012.

Spencer, Richard. "Qatar to Hold National Democratic Elections for the First Time." *The Telegraph* 1 Nov. 2011.

Spencer, Richard. "Qatar to Hold National Democratic Elections for the First Time." *The Telegraph* 1 Nov. 2011.

Totaro, Lorenzo. "Qatar Fund Buys Italy's Costa Smeralda Resort, Sheikh Hamad Says." *Bloomberg* 16 Apr. 2012.

Toumi, Habib. "Qatar's Foreign Workers Overwhelm Labour Market." *The Gulf News* 24 Oct. 2011.

Toumi, Habib. "Qatari Nationals Want Stricter Sponsorship Rules." *Gulf News* 5 Jan. 2011.

Toumi, Habib. "Qatari Women Moving Forward with More Rights, Expert Says." *Gulf News* 22 Dec. 2011.

Watson, Katy. "Libya Conflict: Qatar Tries to Forge a New Global Role." *BBC News* 12 Sept. 2011.

World Finance. "GCC in the Driving Seat." 23 Apr. 2012.

Index